THE ULTIMATE

CARD

TRICK

BOOK

Master the magic of over 70 amazing tricks

EVE DEVEREUX

THE ULTIMATE

CARD

TRICK

BOOK

Master the magic of over 70 amazing tricks

EVE DEVEREUX

CHARTWELL
BOOKS, INC.

A QUINTET BOOK

Published by Chartwell Books
A Division of Book Sales, Inc.
PO Box 7100
Edison, New Jersey 08818-7100

This edition produced for sale in the U.S.A., its
territories and dependencies only.

ISBN 0-7858-0323-8

This book was designed and produced by
Quintet Publishing Limited
6 Blundell Street
London N7 9BH

Creative Director: Richard Dewing
Designer: James Lawrence
Project Editor: Anna Briffa
Editor: Bob Munro
Illustrator: Rob Shone

Typeset in Great Britain by
Central Southern Typesetters, Eastbourne
Manufactured in Hong Kong by Regent Publishing Services Ltd
Printed in China by Leefung-Asco Printers Ltd

Contents

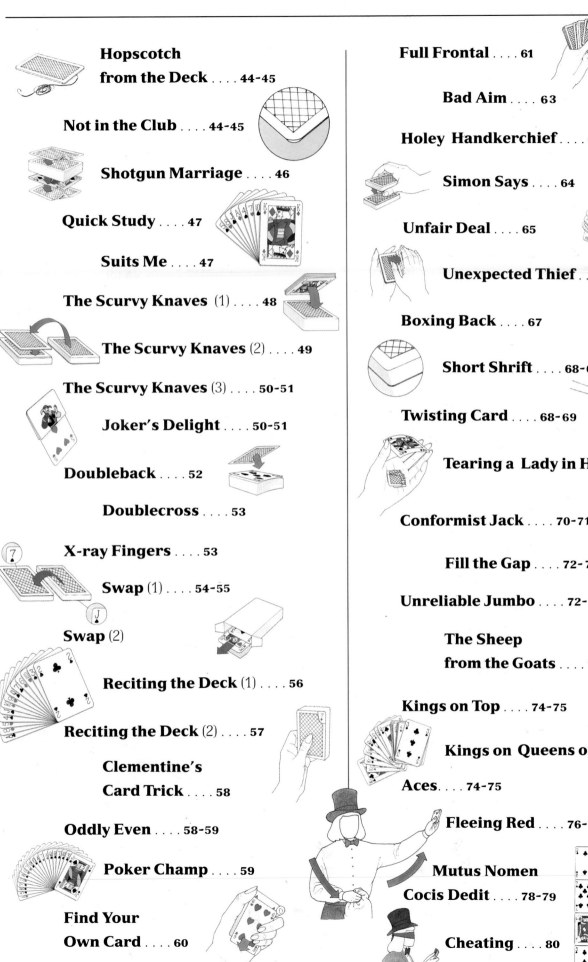
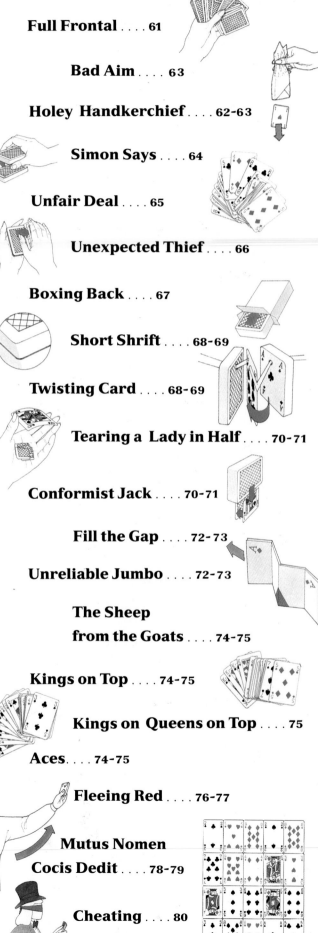

INTRODUCTION

No book can teach you how to be a magician: it can only teach you how to perform tricks. The rest is entirely up to you.

This is because performance magic – conjuring – is really one great big con trick, with the performer being only one of the con-artists involved. The audience know *that you are not using real magic, that you are cheating them in some way, yet they are prepared to maintain the fiction in their own minds that you are using abilities not granted to the mass of humankind. At least, they are prepared to maintain this fiction so long as you present your con tricks with sufficient charm (or, rarely, anti-charm) and vivacity that the audience is persuaded that you are keeping to your side of the unwritten bargain – that you are working hard to entertain them. Successful criminal con-artists have almost always relied on this: they work with sufficient charm and ingenuity that their dupes* want *to believe in them!*

Patter

This is your major aid, especially when performing a routine consisting entirely or largely of card tricks. Cards do not (usually) jump through hoops or burst into flames, or any of the other things that more elaborate magical props can be called upon to do: they are merely immobile pieces of pasteboard, although often enough you will be trying to persuade your audience that they are anything but.

Instead, therefore, you must arrange for all the ostentatious magical effects to be taking place *inside your audience's heads*: you must manipulate their minds – indeed, that is exactly what they *want* you to do.

Your best tool for doing this is patter, which is also your main ally in directing the audience's attention away from things you do not wish them to notice (misdirection). Every card trick can be made to tell a story, and ideally it should be a story that you have invented yourself. I have given an indication of the type of yarn you might tell by giving some of the tricks in this book suitably silly fictitious rationales which you may use in your patter if you wish; other tricks (e.g., the Scurvy Knaves tricks – see pages 48–51) have traditionally had such tales attached to them. Best of all, though, is if you take the basis of a trick, adapt it as you want, and then invent your own story to go along with it.

Also an important part of your patter is the relationship you establish with the audience. Usually you will want to make them laugh, to get them on your side; you can even get them on your side by consistently insulting them, just as long as your insults are witty enough. However, do not be tempted to make humiliating jokes at the expense of those members of the audience you ask to help you (in this book always called volunteers). The volunteers have paid their entrance money just like everyone else, and may have conquered a good deal of nervousness to assist you in front of a hall of spectators, so to hurt their feelings would be unforgivably discourteous. Your audience would soon turn against you – and quite right.

Work on building up the sequence of tricks you want to perform to make a full routine. One line of patter should not end at the finish of one trick, to be replaced by a quite different line at the start of the next. All through the routine, the various elements of your patter should flow naturally into one another. Deciding on a theme is a good way of doing this; a running joke can be helpful.

You

For the purposes of clarity, throughout this book I have assumed that the magician is female and that all the volunteers from the audience are male; in the very few tricks where an accomplice is required, I have again assumed femaleness.

I have also assumed that the magician is right-handed, but on the rare occasions where the directions might be confusing to a left-hander I have indicated as much.

Your choice of dress onstage is something that you will evolve for yourself – it is most likely you will dress differently for different occasions. For most of the tricks it does not matter what you wear; but some of them require pockets or specific garments. Again for the sake of simplicity, I have assumed you will wear trousers (*not* tight ones, like jeans) with standard pockets, an opaque shirt (preferably) or blouse, and a jacket with side and top (breast) pocket. A few tricks require you also to be carrying a handkerchief: this should be large, opaque and – oh yes – clean and freshly ironed. The best way to carry it, unless it would clash entirely with the rest of your presentation, is formally folded in one of the top pockets of your jacket.

Props, Gimmicks and Accomplices

By far the greater majority of the tricks in this book can be done by a solitary performer using standard cards: they can be done anywhere.

For many performances, however, it is desirable to have onstage with you a table and a couple of chairs. For your table a simple folding card-table is perfectly adequate. If you put a tablecloth on it, do not use one that drapes generously to the floor on all sides – that would immediately convince your audience that the table was rigged with all sorts of cunning gadgets and gimmicks, and they would become suspicious every time you approached it. A thin, small tablecloth, of an area about the same as the tabletop but set crosswise on it so that the corners hang, is perfectly sufficient. You might think of using a patterned tablecloth, since on occasion you will indeed be dropping or picking up things that the audience should know nothing about; for the same reason, it is wise if there are a few bits of "clutter" on the table – empty card-boxes, perhaps even a vase of flowers.

The chairs are useful because, especially in intimate venues, many card tricks are best performed when both you and a volunteer are seated on either side of your table.

Employing accomplices can be tiresome and can entirely defeat your purpose. In very many cases the relationship between yourself and the accomplice will be either immediately guessed or already known.

Gimmicks and gadgets can likewise bring down your performance, especially if almost every trick you do relies on them: you know better than anyone else that your assumed cleverness is a complete sham, and this awareness is likely to communicate itself to the audience. Use such artifices sparingly, as I have used them in this book. For your interest, however, I have included a single trick (Hopscotch from the Deck – see pages 44–5) which requires a fairly complicated gadget. Try it – you may find that you are one of those people who actually *prefer* gadget-oriented magic.

The Cards Themselves

Doctored cards – with extra-rounded corners, or with their edges shaved – are another matter: a number of very fine tricks can be done using cards treated in this way, and you will find them (and basic instructions on how to do the doctoring) in a number of tricks in this book. On a few occasions faked or dummied cards can be useful too, and these are likewise described where they occur.

For the most part, however, all you need is a single deck of cards – although preferably you should possess two decks, with matching fronts but different back-designs. Buy the best-quality cards you can sensibly afford: cheap ones are a complete waste of money. Your cards should have a plastic finish, both for durability and so that their surfaces glide easily over each other. It is handy to have an extra deck identical in all respects to one of your two main decks, but with a textured "linen" finish rather than a smooth one.

When one or both of your decks get scruffy through overuse, replace the pair. Do not throw out your old decks, though. Not only can they be useful for practice (better, often, than nice clean new ones), you can cannibalize them for use in making fakes, to replace cards accidentally destroyed, or simply to have an extra copy of a particular card to use in a trick.

Buy cards whose back-designs include a white margin all the way around. Often enough you will want to persuade a volunteer that you are offering him a face-down deck when in fact it is a face-up deck with its topmost card turned face-down. A white margin allows you to splay the deck a little to aid the deception.

Specially faked cards can be bought from conjuring shops, and on occasion they can be useful, though most often you are better off manufacturing your own. For larger venues you might think of buying Jumbo Cards (also known as Giant Cards), but these are extremely expensive and can be used for only a limited repertoire of tricks – imagine trying to shuffle a deck of Jumbo Cards!

One special type of cards is worth considering. If your hands are small, you may find it difficult to do many of these tricks using a standard deck. Try them again using a deck of patience (solitaire) cards. These little cards are generally very attractive, largely just because of their smallness, and you could make the fact that you use them a distinctive and appealing feature of your act.

Practice!

Yes: do. It is an old adage of magic that you should practice any trick until you know it thoroughly, then until you can do it every time perfectly without even thinking about it, and then a bit more so that you can do it better than that!

BELOW: The Riffle Shuffle (see page 16). Once mastered, this shuffle is both efficient and impressive. It will add a hint of professionalism to your routine.

THE
TRICKS

♣ STRAIGHT SHUFFLE

This is the shuffle which most of us ordinarily use when playing with cards.

The deck starts in the left hand, with the cards facing towards the inside of the hand (i.e., towards the ball of the thumb). The fingers and thumb of the right hand grip the ends of most of the deck, lifting it up so that a small packet remains in the left hand. The right hand then drops a few cards into the left on the inside of this packet, then a few to its outside, then a few on the inside, and so on until all the cards are once more in the left hand.

This shuffle is open to various deceptions, for all of which you should have the basic shuffle sufficiently practiced that you can do it very quickly and easily and that no one watching can really keep track of the cards.

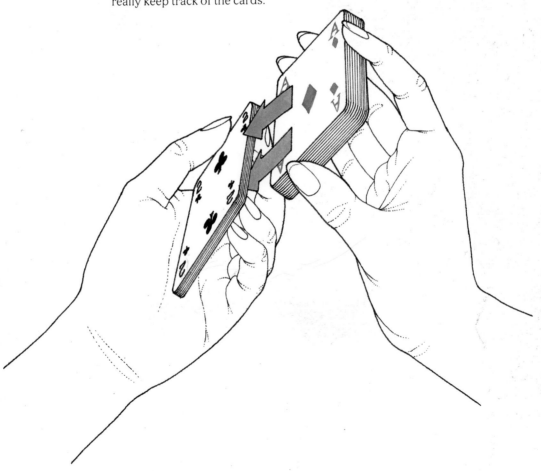

♥ STRAIGHT-SHUFFLE DECEPTIONS

The straight shuffle is more open to simple fakery than any other type of shuffle, with the possible exception of the Hindoo Shuffle (see pages 18–19).

a) It is easy to keep the original top card of the deck at the top. You simply ensure that the final few cards are dropped from the right hand always to the rear of the packet in the left hand. Similarly, you can keep several cards at the top of the deck, in order – up to as many as 15 or even 20.

b) You can likewise keep the deck's bottom card or cards at the bottom. Merely start the shuffle with the cards facing not inward toward the ball of the left hand's thumb, but outward, facing away from it.

c) You can in fact not shuffle the cards at all. Although you go through all the motions of an ordinary shuffle, in fact you consistently drop the cards from the right hand *behind* the growing packet in the left hand. You cannot hope to get away with this every time if you perform the maneuver directly in front of the audience, but it can be handy to know you can do it while turning away or while distracting the audience's attention elsewhere – simply to add to the illusion that you really are shuffling the cards thoroughly.

d) You can shuffle a card from the bottom of the deck to the top. In your first pick-up with the right hand, leave only a single card in the left. For a preliminary shuffle, always drop the cards on the inside of the growing packet in the left hand. Immediately start a second shuffle, to disguise the paucity of this first one, this time shuffling normally except retaining the new top card in its place.

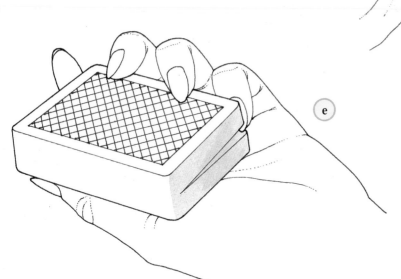

e) You can shuffle a card from the center of the deck to the top, assuming that you have located the card through having made a break in the deck (perhaps with a fingernail). Here the first packet you pick up with the right hand contains all the cards down to the break (i.e., not including the chosen card). Your procedure is then as per **d**.

f) You can use a shuffle to arrange that there is a face-up card at the bottom of a face-down deck. **i)** At the end of an orthodox shuffle, wrap the fingers of the left hand around the deck to grip the last card. **ii)** Pick up the rest of the deck with the right hand, and at once seemingly use both hands simply to square up the deck.

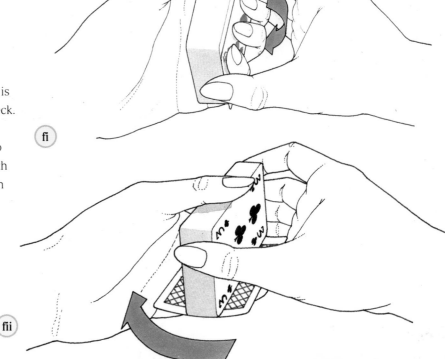

15

♠ RIFFLE SHUFFLE

The riffle shuffle is another that is frequently used when playing card games.

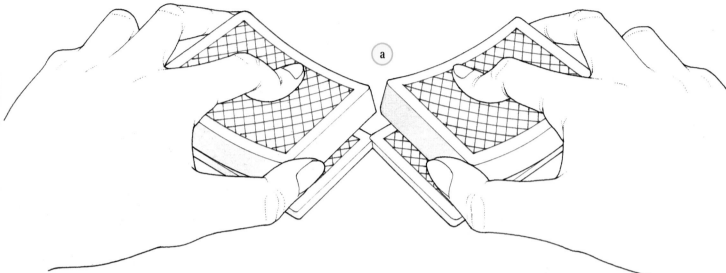

a) You cut the deck into two packets, place both face-down on a flat surface with their corners adjacent, bend the corners up with the thumbs, move the two packets still closer together, and release the cards such that the corners of the two packets interlock with a satisfying riffling sound. You then use both hands to merge the two packets, so that the deck is restored with its cards thoroughly rearranged. Alternatively, you can make the shorter edges of the two packets overlap, rather than just the corners. This variant is often called the dovetail shuffle.

b) Rather more difficult is the riffle shuffle performed without recourse to a flat surface. The two packets face toward each other as you start, one in each hand, the cards being held between the thumbs and the first joints of the fingers. Bring the index finger of each hand around and press its back against the rear of the respective packet; then bring the thumbs closer together and riffle the ends of the cards into each other. You may require a deal of practice to master this – and you may not consider the practice worth it, since the two simpler techniques look better.

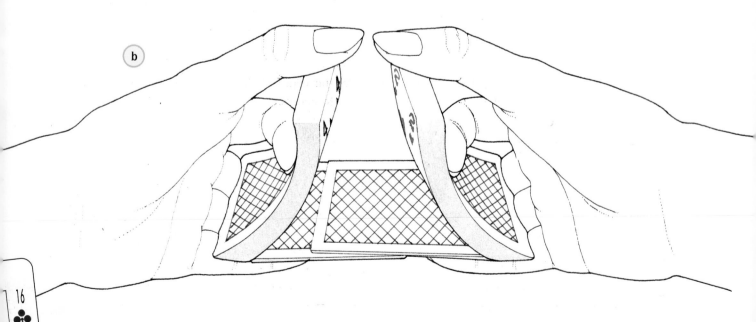

◆ PALMING

There are two principal techniques of
palming used in card tricks, one of them
involving the palm of the hand and the other,
confusingly (and much less usefully), not.
Both are designed to make it possible for you
to have cards in your hand when the
audience believes your hands to be empty.

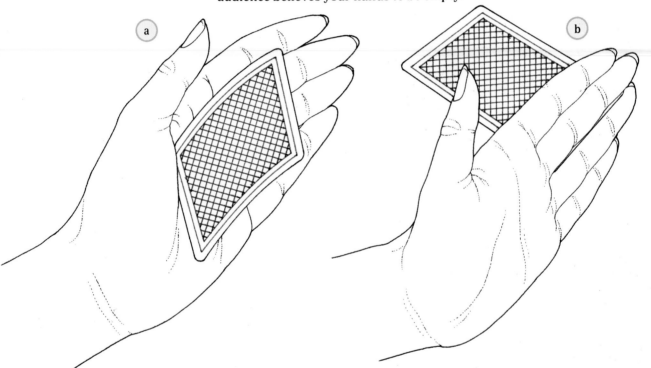

a) A card can be held on the inside of the hand, curved into the palm and braced, usually, between the ball of the thumb and the second joints of the fingers. The exact location of the upper end of the card will depend on the size of your hands. People with big hands will have it braced against the second joints of all four fingers (or even against the base of the fingers); those with smaller hands can brace the edge against the second joints of the three fingers other than the index finger; and so forth. Practice until you find out exactly the position that suits you. If your hands are very small, try the exercise using a patience (solitaire) card: you may find it better to use such cards for all tricks that require palming. Now practice palming the top card from the deck so easily that it looks as if your hand has merely glided over the surface. You might also try palming more than one card at a time.

b) The other technique allows you to display the open face of your hand to the audience, showing it to be empty, when in fact you are holding a card. The card is held, by one of its short ends, between the second and third fingers and almost all of it sticks out at the back of the hand; the thin edge of card does not show between the fingers, either because of the line between them already naturally there or because their flesh touches in front of the card's edge, obscuring it. It is not at all difficult to hold cards in this way – what is difficult is actually getting them there in the first place. None of the tricks in this book use this palming technique, which is included here solely for the sake of completeness: the most likely result of your attempting to use it is that you drop or show the card at the most embarrassing possible moment, thereby destroying the effect of the trick.

17

♣ HINDOO SHUFFLE

This method of shuffling is rarely used in playing card games, but is more widely employed by magicians, since it looks slick and allows for deceptions that are not possible with other shuffles. It requires a lot of practice, so you must decide for yourself whether the effort is worth it.

At the start, the deck is held horizontally face-down by the fingers and thumb of the right hand.

Advance the deck toward the cupped left hand, and grip the top cards of the deck between its fingers and thumb, with the index finger moved around the end of the received deck for purposes of control (if it is not there, you are soon going to be throwing cards all over the floor – enough of a danger anyway when learning the shuffle). The right hand takes the bulk of the deck away from beneath this top packet, which you let fall from

♥ THE PASS

The object of the Pass is to bring a card to the top or bottom of the deck unknown to the audience. Typically you will have asked a volunteer to pick a card and then return it to the center of the proffered deck. There are two common methods whereby you can then immediately bring that card to the top.

(a)

hands, it is easy with the right hand to displace the two packets just a trifle sideways from each other as he is pushing his card toward it. The card in place, swiftly begin to give the deck a straight shuffle, beginning by cutting the deck at the position of your fingernail so that the selected card is brought to the top.

b) The first technique requires only a little practice; the second is much more difficult. **i)** As the card is inserted, the fingers of your left hand, holding the deck, should crimp the sides of the packet beneath that card, putting a slight bend on those cards, so that the two packets become quite distinct from each other. **ii)** The middle fingers of your left hand can then reach across the top of the deck to pull the upper packet sideways away from the lower. **iii)** As if you were merely tidying the cards, you then use the fingers of your right hand further to separate the packets, forcing the edges of the lower packet into the base of the left

a) This involves your having at least one long fingernail on the hand in which you hold the deck, preferably on the little finger of the left hand. Although the volunteer thinks he is putting the selected card back into a random place in the deck, in fact, hidden from his view by the cards, you have already inserted your fingernail into the deck's rear corner, splitting it into two packets. As you offer the deck to him with both your

(bi)

18
♠

the left hand's fingers toward the cupped palm as the right hand advances the deck to repeat the process.

As noted, a well executed Hindoo shuffle looks slick, because it is *obviously* a difficult maneuver. For that same reason, no one will be surprised if the amassed cards in your left hand look a bit sloppy. This leaves the way open for one of the

deceptions possible with this shuffle. At any stage during the shuffle you can irritably use the cards still remaining in the right hand to tap those in the left into better order, and this gives you the opportunity to glimpse the bottom card of the packet in the right hand. It is clearly simple thereafter to make sure that this card becomes the top card in the deck when the shuffle is completed.

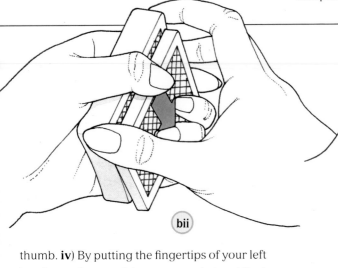

thumb. **iv**) By putting the fingertips of your left hand over the top of the upper packet and flexing the thumb as you close your left hand, you can bring the lower packet over the upper. **v**) This brings the selected card to either the top or the bottom of the deck, depending on whether you chose to crimp it as part of the lower packet or leave it as part of the upper.

You must be prepared to put in a lot of practice if you are to get the latter technique right, so that you can perform it smoothly and quickly enough for it to be undetectable to the volunteer, who is likely still to be close in front of you. You should also practice it for transferring just a single card from bottom to top of the deck – this is perhaps its most useful application. Don't be discouraged if you keep dropping the cards all over the floor in your early attempts: most people do. Your aim is to become so accustomed to the maneuver that it is almost instinctive, so practice on boring train journeys or anywhere else that you have time – and cards – on your hands. If your hands are big enough, you may find that you can eventually execute the Pass one-handed.

You should also try adapting both of these techniques – particularly **a** – so that you can allow volunteers to return their cards to a fanned deck.

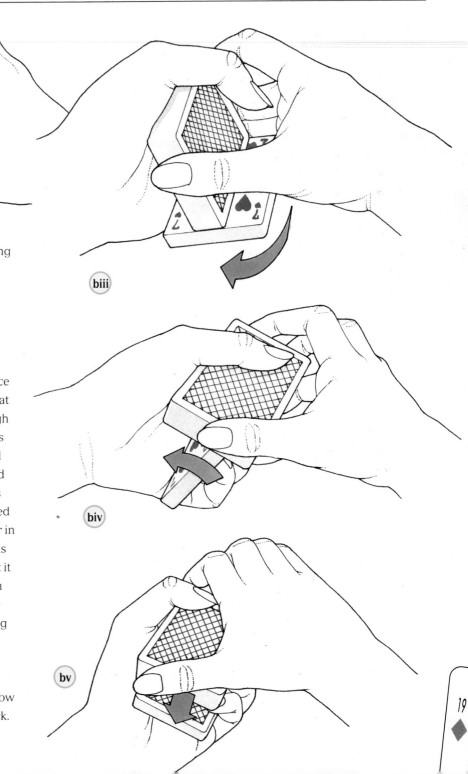

♠ FORCING A CARD (1)

The object of all techniques of forcing cards is to make a volunteer think that he has selected a card at random, whereas in fact the one that he has chosen has been predetermined by you.

The simplest method of forcing is also the most fallible, and you should use it only when you are certain of your audience; ideally they should be casual and laughing, already convinced by other tricks that you are more or less infallible – even better if you are performing at a party or in a bar, so that everyone has had a few drinks. All you do, while fanning out the deck or immediately afterward, is to edge forward a little with your thumbnail or thumb the predetermined card – which should be roughly in the center of those that you have fanned out. (Note that, in fanning out a complete deck, you need only proffer the central cards of the deck with the others to either side being more bunched up.) A casual volunteer will probably opt for the card that is protruding slightly from the rest; if not, it is easy enough casually to rotate your wrists a little to bring the predetermined card gradually under his descending fingers.

If still unsuccessful, suddenly "remember" some part of the trick you have forgotten to set up, and retreat to your table. Either try this technique of forcing on a different member of the audience, or, preferably, use one of the alternatives described below.

◆ FORCING A CARD (2): The Bridge

Your predetermined card is at the bottom of the deck. Cut the deck yourself first, crimping the (original) upper packet as you do so to form a bridge. As you complete the cut, therefore, there will be a distinct gap between the upper and lower packets. Offer the deck in your hand to the volunteer and ask him to cut the deck. If you do this quickly and offhandedly enough, he will

invariably cut at the gap, and thereby at your predetermined card.

You can do this at your table rather than offering the deck in your hand. However, this is much more risky. Not only are you giving the volunteer much more time to think, and hence to cut at somewhere other than the obvious place, you are also not in control of which way he habitually takes the cards when cutting a deck – most people grip the cards at the sides but some grip them at the ends – and consequently you may have crimped the bridge in the wrong direction – widthways when it should have been lengthways, or vice versa. By offering the cards in your hand you determine the way the volunteer cuts the deck, whatever his normal practice.

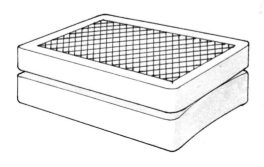

♣ FORCING A CARD (3): The Riffle Force

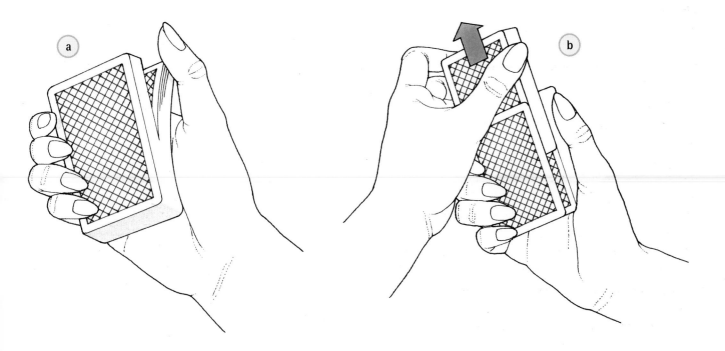

a) The predetermined card is at the top of the deck. Holding the deck face-down in your right hand, with your fingers wrapped around it, riffle one corner of the exposed end with your thumb. Do this a few times through the deck, and then ask the volunteer to stop you at any time mid-riffle. When he does so, reach across with your left hand and remove the cards of the upper packet, offering him the lower packet, the top card of which is the one his call has selected.

b) In fact, when drawing the upper packet away from the lower, the tips of the wrapped-around fingers of your right hand have pressed against the back of the top card so that, as you drew the packet away, that card stayed in your right hand and fell naturally onto the lower packet. With a little rehearsal you will find you can perform the whole maneuver so swiftly and naturally that it is undetectable.

In practice, the right hand's fingertips often retain two or three cards rather than just the top one, but of course this does not matter – and with practice you can use this to your advantage in order to force more than one card simultaneously.

♥ FORCING A CARD (4): Cut it Yourself

This is a very simple way of forcing either one or a pair of cards on a volunteer. Ask him to cut the deck wherever he wants, and then either you or he can lay the ex-bottom half of the deck crosswise over the top. Because of his participation, the volunteer believes the two crossed cards at the new center of the deck have been randomly selected; in fact, of course, they are the cards that were originally at the top and bottom of the deck.

You want to perform this force quickly and with the maximum of distracting patter.

♠ FORCING A CARD (5): Deal it Yourself

The predetermined card is at the top of the deck. To show the selection process is truly random, keep shuffling the deck, ensuring that you retain the predetermined card in its place, while asking the volunteer to think of any number between 1 and 52. When he has done so, stop shuffling, and tell him you want him to count off the cards from the top of the deck until he reaches that number – demonstrate this yourself to make it absolutely clear what you want him to do: if his number was 17, count off 16 cards and show him the 17th (which is, of course, of no interest). Put the 17th card on top of the heap you have counted off and then return this heap to the top of the deck. Pass the deck to him and ask him to repeat the exercise. Obviously, because of your "demonstration", the card that started at the top of the deck is now the 17th down from the top.

♦ FORCING A CARD (6): Shuffle-Stop

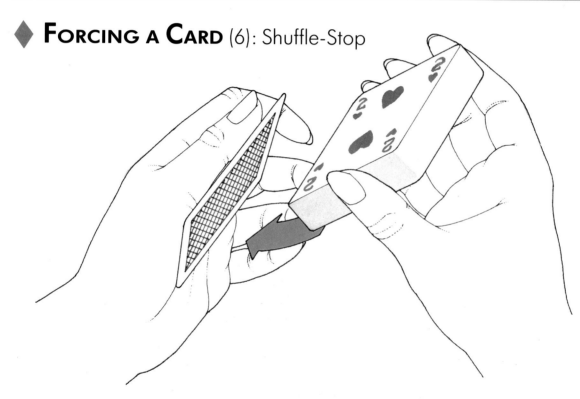

The predetermined card can start either at the top or at the bottom of your deck. You tell the volunteer that you want him to call out at any moment while you are shuffling. The shuffle you perform looks like a normal straight shuffle (see page 13), but in fact it is a close variant. If the predetermined card has started at the top of the deck, perform a straight shuffle to take it to the bottom. For the variant shuffle you use from here on, pick off a packet not from the outside of the deck but from the inside (i.e., from the side of the deck closer to the ball of your thumb). The cards you then drop to either side of the new central cluster come in groups from the rear, not the front, of this packet, so that the bottom few cards of the packet are retained firmly between your fingertips until, at last, you drop them at the bottom of the deck. Repeat this over and over while telling the volunteer what you want him to do. Whatever time he calls out to you to stop, the face-out card at the bottom of the packet in your upper hand will always be the one you selected in advance.

Practice this variant of the straight shuffle: it is much easier than it sounds. It can be tricky with new cards or with excessively old and greasy ones, so use a worn deck both in practice and for the performance.

♣ CARD PHOTOGRAPHY

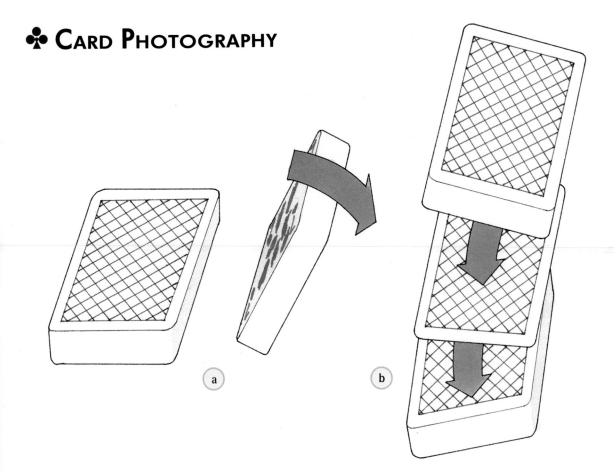

a

b

Effect: The magician asks a volunteer to select a card from the deck and to show it to the rest of the audience but not to the magician, who is in the meantime cutting the deck on her table. The card returned, the magician places it in the center of the cut deck, which she then shuffles. She now tells the audience that cards can sometimes act like a temporary photographic film, retaining for a short while the last image to which they were exposed. Turning up the cards one by one, she at last pounces on a card, declaring that she can see the volunteer's features clearly on its face. She rushes to show him, but of course by this time the image has faded in the light – though it is indeed his card.

Method: This is a basic trick dressed up in misleading patter.

a) All you must do is peep at the bottom of the deck – either before starting or while the volunteer is examining his selection – so that you know the identity of the card there (e.g., the Seven of Spades).

b) When you return the volunteer's card to the cut deck, you place it on the pile that was earlier the top half of the deck; setting the other half on top of this obviously brings the Seven of Spades to the position directly over the selected card. You then give the deck a fake shuffle or two and start turning up the cards. The next one after the Seven of Spades is, of course, the one you seek.

> **TIP**
> Without the patter, this technique can be used as part of other tricks any time you need to know the location of a card selected by a volunteer.

23

♦

♥ THE SPIRITS SPEAK

Effect: The magician fans out the deck, face-down, on her table and tells the audience that the spirits will guide a handful of the people from the front row in their selection of cards. Calling up the first volunteer, she asks him to tap the back of the card he thinks is (say) the Ace of Hearts; pulling out this card she announces that the selection has been accurate, then asks another volunteer to choose (e.g.,) the Seven of Diamonds. This carries on until a handful of volunteers have each picked out a card; finally the magician herself chooses a card (e.g., the Three of Spades). The magician then gives each of the volunteers the card to which the spirits guided his finger.

♠ THE VAIN CARD (1)

Effect: The magician asks a volunteer to pick a card from the deck, show it to his companions, and then return it. While shuffling the deck, she explains to the audience that cards can be as guilty of the minor sins as human beings are – and especially of the sin of vanity. In particular, the card that was selected has become overly proud of the fact that it was chosen from among the other 51 – indeed, there is nothing the magician can do to stop it rising from the middle of the deck to accept the audience's applause.

a) Holding the deck up towards the audience, she watches along with them as the selected card slowly and mysteriously emerges . . .

Method: As soon as the card is returned to the deck, use either version of the Pass (see pages 18–19) to bring it to the top. The shuffle is of course a fake. When you display the "shuffled" deck to the audience with the selected card at its rear, hold the deck between your thumb on one side and your third and little fingers on the other.

b) This leaves your middle two fingers behind the deck, hidden from view, and you can use them simply to "walk" the card slowly upwards. To the audience, a little distance from you, it looks as if the card is emerging from somewhere in the centre of the deck, an illusion you have reinforced with your patter.

a

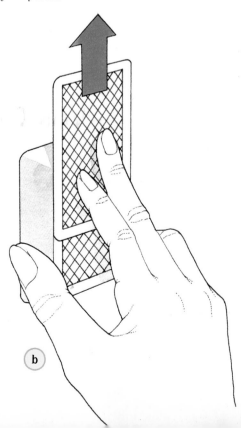

b

Method: At the start, you must ensure – using any of the standard methods – that you know where in the deck of cards the Ace of Hearts is sited. If the card chosen by the first volunteer, on his being asked to let the spirits guide him to the Ace of Hearts, proves to be the Seven of Diamonds, then that is the card you ask the next volunteer to find. After this routine has been repeated five or six times, you announce that you yourself will pick up the final card. If the card selected by the last volunteer was the Three of Spades, that is the card you say the spirits are guiding you to. You in fact pick up the Ace of Hearts, thereby completing the set.

TIP

If, by bad luck, it is the first or second volunteer who chooses the Ace of Hearts, you should instantly display the card(s), saying that this was merely a demonstration to make sure the rest of the audience understood what was going on.

♦ THE VAIN CARD (2)

Effect: In the customary way, the magician invites a volunteer to select a card and examine it, and then to return it to the deck. Cards, explains the magician as she shuffles, are as vain as human beings, and she knows for a fact that this particular card will now consider itself superior to all its fellows. As proof, she fans out the deck face-down, and sure enough the selected card has turned itself the opposite way from the rest, so that it shows face-up.

Method: While the volunteer is looking at his card, showing it to those around him, etc., you simply turn over the bottom card of the deck, so it is face-down against the face of the next card (see page 15 for one way of doing this). When you proffer the deck to the volunteer for him to push his card into it, therefore, the deck looks face-down when in fact all the cards except the top one are face-up. Your only problem now is to turn the deceiving card back the way it was, which you can do in the course of performing the shuffle.

TIP

This trick is best done in conjunction with the previous one. It is advisable not to repeat it, because someone is sure to cotton on to what's happening if you do it too many times.
You can adapt the patter of the next trick to make it a brief flourish to conclude a set of three tricks involving the vanity of cards.

♣ I'm It!

Effect: The magician shows the audience the top card of the deck (e.g., the Ten of Spades) and explains that this card is often found at the top of the deck because of its notorious vanity. She pushes the card into the center of the deck, puts the deck on her table, claps her hands above it and demonstrates that the Ten of Spades is once again at the top.

Method: This trick depends on the speed with which you can make the second version of the Pass (see pages 18–19) to bring a single card from the bottom of the deck to the top.

Take the first card from the top of the deck (e.g., the Ten of Spades) and, having shown it around, return it to its place as if absent-mindedly. While continuing your patter ("Funny thing about the Ten of Spades, incidentally . . . Look, I'll show you"), swiftly Pass the bottom card of the deck up to the top. Without showing the audience its face, take what is now the top card (which they will assume still to be the Ten of Spades) and push it at random into the deck. The trick is done, although it will be a while before the audience knows this.

A simpler variant relies on the little fingernail of your left hand being long enough.

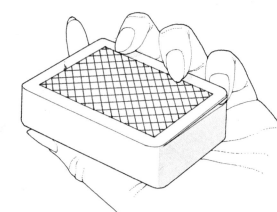

a

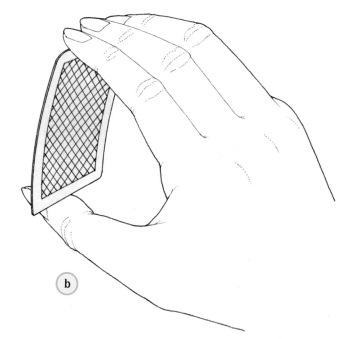

b

a) With that hand holding the deck, slip the nail under the second-top card.

b) When showing the audience the "top" card, in fact peel off both the first and second together, as if they were just a single card. Return the two cards to the top of the deck; it is the single top card that you then push into the deck.

TIP

The first version of this trick can be done as a finale after the preceding two. Take the card that has already demonstrated its vanity twice (e.g., the Ten of Spades) and put it on top of the deck. As if on an afterthought, address some taunting remark toward it (by now you have already made the Pass) to the effect that *this* time it is going to be lost in obscurity. Matching actions to words, draw off the top card and push it into the deck. Then, looking annoyed, peel off the new top card and show that the Ten of Spades has, apparently, returned immediately to its preeminent position. You can do this two or three times, very quickly (practice!), getting crosser and crosser, before abandoning the whole thing as a lost cause.

♥ RED UNDER THE BED

Effect: The magician deals out six cards, alternately face-down and face-up. She writes down a prediction on a sheet of paper which she folds up and tucks into the pocket of a volunteer. She then asks him to think of any number between 1 and 6, picks up the card thus indicated and asks him to read the prediction from his pocket. It says: "You will pick the only red card out of the six." Which is what he did.

Method: Only two cards are important: a Six of either Hearts or Diamonds, and the Ace of either Spades or Clubs. The Ace is drawn from a deck with a red design on the back; the other five cards are from a non-red-backed deck. Aside from the two specified cards, the remainder can have any value other than 1–6 and be a mixture of Spades and Clubs. The order of cards at the top of the deck before you deal is: Other, Ace, Six, Other, Other, Other. Lay these out face-down, face-up, face-down, face-up, face-down, face-up. If the volunteer picks the number 1, you swoop on the Ace and show that it alone has a red back; if 2, you count left to right to get the Ace again; if 3, count the same way to get the Six; if 4, count right to left to get the Six; if 5, count that way to get the Ace; if 6, pick up the Six. It's all a swindle, of course, but that won't seem evident at the time.

TIP

Face the volunteer across the table while performing this trick: that way, counting left to right will not seem so unnatural – you can even ask him to do the counting. Never be tempted to encore this trick!

♠ YOUR CARD IS

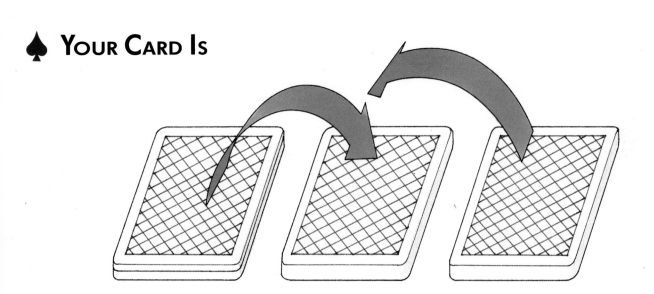

Effect: The magician deals out three packets, each of seven cards, and puts the rest of the deck to one side. She then asks a volunteer to pick up any one of the three packets and to mentally select one of the cards in it. She then takes up all three packets and deals them out again into three new packets of seven cards. She asks the volunteer to pick up each packet in turn to find which one contains the chosen card. Again she gathers the cards, again she deals out three packets, and again the volunteer informs her which of them contains his card. Collecting the cards once more, the magician spells off from the top of the complete packet, removing one card for each letter, the phrase Y-O-U-R C-A-R-D I-S – and the next card is indeed the one he chose.

Method: The secret of this trick lies in the order in which you pick up the packets: each time, the packet containing the chosen card should be between the other two packets. If you do this, the trick works itself.

TIP

You can add to the effect by asking the volunteer to do most of the work himself – all you have to do is hand him the packets each time, to make sure that they are gathered in the correct order. As he spells off the cards at the end, ask him to spell out H-E-R-E-'S M-Y C-A-R-D, and the card corresponding to the "d" will indeed be his.

◆ COUNTING CARDS (1)

Effect: The magician counts out a number of cards from the top of the deck while remarking to the audience that the power of magic is present in everyone's mind, but that in most cases it is unrealized. Returning the dealt cards to the deck, she adds that, for example, everybody present has the subconscious knowledge of where in the deck every card is – for example, the Ten of Hearts. To prove this, she asks someone to give her a number between 10 and 20 (e.g., 17).

a) She then counts cards out as before, this time 17 of them. Putting the rest of the deck to one side, she picks up the packet of 17 cards and adds the digits of the number 17 together: 1 + 7 = 8.

b) She then deals eight cards from the top of the packet, the eighth of which is indeed the Ten of Hearts.

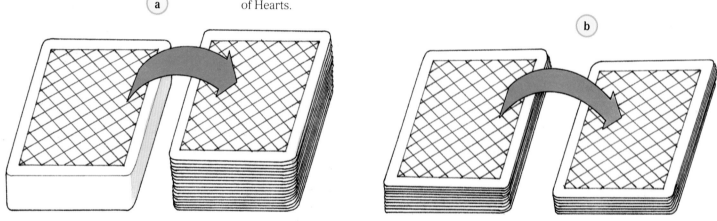

a

b

Method: This is a self-working trick. The number of cards you deal at the outset is in fact 10, although there is no need to draw attention to this fact: either you can do the counting *sotto voce* or you can count as far as 11 and stop just before you drop that card onto the heap. Either way, as you return the heap to the deck, catch a glimpse of its bottom card – e.g., the Ten of Hearts. Thereafter there is no deception.

TIP

The trick obviously does not work if the number selected is 20, but it would seem artificial to request a number between 10 and 19. It is very unlikely that the volunteer will select 20 but, if he does, you can simply stress that you asked for a number *between* 10 and 20. Alternatively, you can ask the audience as a whole for the number, and simply "not hear" any calls for 20.

♣ COUNTING CARDS (2)

Effect: The magician gives a volunteer a set of nine cards, running from Ace to Nine in mixed suits, turns her back, and asks him to lay them out in three rows. He is then asked to select any one of the cards and remove it from the array. She next asks him to think of the cards in each row as digits making up a three-figure number – e.g., a row showing Four, Eight and Six would be regarded as 486 – and to add up the three rows, with the gap where he removed a card being counted as a 0. Once he has completed the addition, he must tot up the digits of the total and give her the answer. Still with her back turned, she tells him immediately the card he chose.

Method: Determining the numerical value of the chosen card is easy: you simply subtract the volunteer's final total from either 9 (if less than 9), 18 (if between 9 and 17) or 27 (if 18 or greater). A simple mathematical principle determines that the result of your subtraction is the correct numerical value. The secret of the card's identity is that, while the suits of the nine cards *seem* random, in fact they are not: you set them up beforehand. There are various mnemonics you can use to remember what they are. An easy one is to think of the order of precedence of the suits in games like bridge: Spades, Hearts, Diamonds, Clubs. The first two suits represent odd numbers, the second pair even numbers. As Spades are superior to Hearts, they represent more numbers: 1 (Ace), 5 and 9 are Spades, while the intervening odd numbers, 3 and 7, are Hearts. Following a similar line of reasoning, 2 and 6 are Diamonds and 4 and 8 are Clubs.

TIP

This trick can be repeated three or four times, with your back still turned and with different volunteers laying out the cards in any ordering of three rows of three, and becomes more impressive with the repetition. Do not use too simple a mnemonic; for example, someone might notice if all the black cards were odd and all the red ones even.

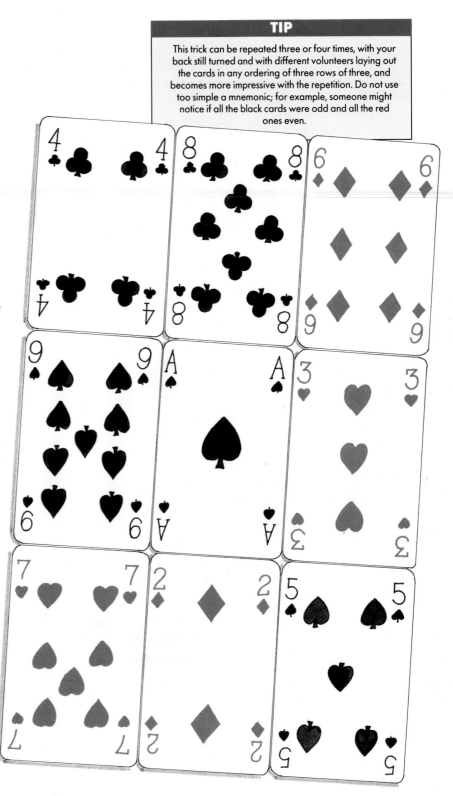

♥ COUNTING CARDS (3)

Effect: The magician deals off the top 10 cards from the deck, face-up, and asks a volunteer to count the numerical value of the cards (with Jack = 11, Queen = 12 and King = 13). While he is announcing the total to the rest of the audience, the magician returns the cards to the deck and repeats the process with the next 10 cards from the top. When these are added up they give a different total. This time, while the volunteer is adding up the figures and announcing the result, the magician is writing something on a sheet of paper, which she folds and passes to a different member of the audience. Taking back the second packet from the volunteer, she tells him that what she has written down is a prediction of the total of 10 cards that he himself will deal. She cuts the deck at random, hands him the lower packet, and he counts out 10 cards, then tots up their value. His result is 70, and this proves to be the number the magician wrote down.

Method: This trick requires a stacked deck. Separate the Twos, Sevens and Queens from the rest of the pack. Take one numerical set from the remainder, in mixed suits, and lay it out in a shuffled row; for example, Three, Five, Jack, King, Nine, Ace, Four, Six, Eight, Ten. From the remaining 30 cards, choose another numerical set in mixed suits and lay it out in a row below the first one, following the same random order. Do this two more times and then collect up the rows as four packets to make a deck of 40 cards. Thoroughly shuffle the 12 cards you earlier discarded and put them at the top of the deck. Once the first 10 cards have been counted, use the volunteer announcing the total to cover the fact that you are not returning all of the cards to the top of the deck – only about half of them, with the remainder going to the bottom. The second time, put the whole packet of 10 back on top of the deck. Thereafter the trick works itself.

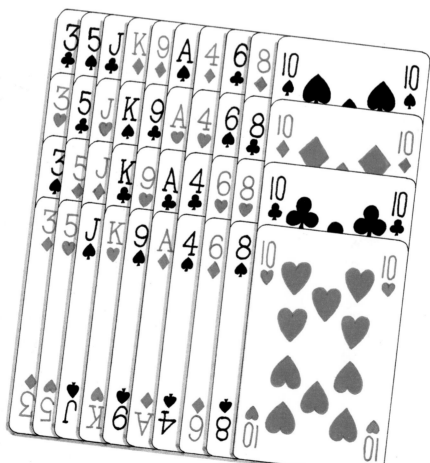

TIP

Between different performances you can vary the total by excluding a different trio of numbers – for example, if you discarded the Twos, Eights and Queens rather than the Twos, Sevens and Queens, the total of the volunteer's cards would always be 69. You can add to the effect by allowing the volunteer to make the cut himself, relying on the fact that he will almost certainly cut the deck somewhere near the middle. If he does not, immediately grab the cards from him on some pretext (e.g., it's a new deck and the cards may be sticking together – no, everything seems all right), and then return the deck. It is extremely unlikely that he will be so perverse a second time.

♠ THE WHITE RABBIT'S CARD TRICK

Effect: Explaining that this was a trick taught to Alice by the White Rabbit, but that Alice forgot about it when telling Lewis Carroll of her adventures, the magician asks four volunteers to choose cards, and then asks them to decide among themselves which one of those four they like the best. While they are discussing the matter, the magician deals the rest of the deck into two equal packets.

a) Receiving back the cards, but not looking at them, she asks the volunteers to select which packet they would like the chosen card to be placed on; then she asks them which packet they'd like the other three cards to be placed on.

b) This done, she puts one packet on top of the other, glances at her watch (which is what the White Rabbit did when showing the trick to Alice) and announces the time – e.g., 5:23. She asks one of the volunteers to add these two numbers to give her the result – 28 – and obediently counts down through the deck to reveal that the 28th card is indeed the chosen one.

Method: This trick works itself, but can be performed only at certain times of day – 12:16, 1315, 1:27, 1414, 2:26, 1513, 3:25, 1612, 4:24, 1711. 5:23, 1810, 6:22, 1909, 7:21, 2008, 8:20, 2107, 9:19, 2206, 10:18, 2305 and 11:17. (In fact, it can be done at any time within a couple of minutes of one of these, because you're the person who checks your watch, and for all the audience knows it may be a little fast or slow.) So long as it is always the packet on which the chosen card was *not* placed that is set on top of the other, the chosen card will always be the 28th from the top. The beauty of this trick is that the option presented to the volunteers of choosing which packet to place the cards on seems to prevent any prior calculation by you of the position of the card, whereas in fact – as a little thought reveals – it makes no difference to the position whatsoever.

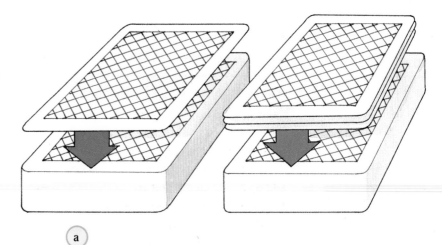

a

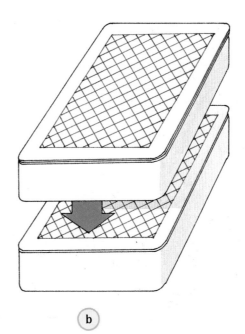

b

> ### TIP
> Depending on the size of your audience, you can have the volunteers select from among not four but six or eight cards. (The trick does not work with an odd number of cards.) With six cards the chosen one will end up 29th from the top, with eight cards 30th. Obviously, you must recalculate the time of your performance accordingly. With a big audience you could give out even more cards (16, say, in which case the card would be 34th down) and organize a game between different groups of the audience to determine the final choice; however, you must be confident of your ability to control the audience so that the game ends at about the desired time.

◆ FLYING CARDS (1)

Effect: The magician is able to throw a card, accurately and quickly, to a member of the audience. In fact, she is able to do this several times in quick succession, each time to a different member of the audience.

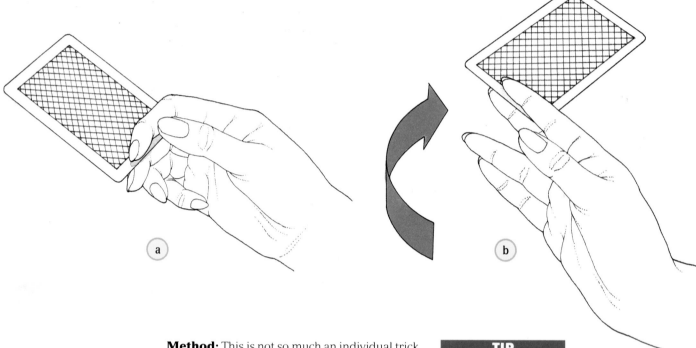

a

b

Method: This is not so much an individual trick as an embellishment that you can use at any stage of your performance. In fact, there is no deception involved: merely the acquisition of the knack.

a) The technique is to hold the card with one of its shorter edges between the first and second fingers of your hand.

b) To throw it, you extend your arm suddenly while at the same time giving the card a backward flick out of your fingers so that it skims horizontally through the air; the movement as a whole is much the same as if you were hitting a backhand shot in table tennis. The first few times you try this, the card will merely flutter in the air in front of you, but sooner or later – it may be on your third attempt, it may not come for half an hour – you will suddenly find that you manage to throw the card perfectly. Practice for a little longer and you'll be able to get it right every time.

TIP

New cards work better than worn ones. You can also try holding the card between thumb and first finger, to see if that suits you better. Either way, do be careful that you don't throw the card too hard: it is traveling through the air at a fair speed and also rotating horizontally as it goes, so if you were unlucky it could cut someone's face.

♣ FLYING CARDS (2)

Effect: A card is selected in the customary way, and then returned to the deck. The magician starts throwing cards toward the audience, to show that she is performing with a perfectly standard deck; apparently to the surprise of the magician as much as anyone else, one card pauses over the heads of the audience and comes back to her. This proves to be the chosen card.

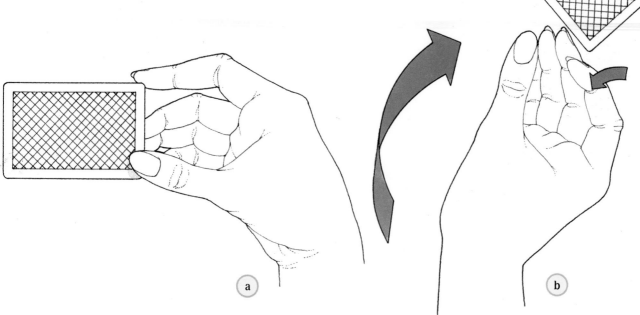

a

b

Method: Use the Pass (see pages 18–19) and a straight shuffle (see page 13) to get the selected card to the bottom of the deck. Throw the first few cards from the top of the deck using the technique outlined for the previous trick. Once you feel you have done this enough, choose as your next card the one from the bottom (i.e., the selected card). This you must grip a little differently:

a) Hold the near corner of one of its shorter sides between your thumb and all fingertips except that of the index finger; the index fingertip rests on the corner further away from you.

b) Your throw this time is not horizontal but upward at an angle of about 45 degrees; moreover, you throw more gently. As you release the card, give it a flick with the index fingertip. When the card reaches the top of its arc it will come spinning back toward you.

TIP

This trick requires even more practice than the preceding one. Don't be deterred if it seems impossible at first, although you might like to try holding the card along one of its longer, rather than shorter, sides to see if this suits you better. Once you have mastered the basic knack, you should practice in front of a mirror to make sure that your throwing action is indistinguishable from the normal one. And, of course, you should practice *catching* the card as well!

♥ FLYING CARDS (3)

Effect: The magician asks a volunteer to choose a card, which is then returned to the deck. While it is being shown around in the usual way, the magician explains how playing cards have often reminded her of pigeons, except that – for the obvious reason that cards have no brains *at all* – it is more difficult to teach them to "home". She encourages the volunteer and his friends to inculcate the principle into the chosen card by singing to it a piece of doggerel – e.g., "You're the cleverest playing

card in the pack, so show us you are by flying right back." After they have made fools of themselves for long enough, the card is returned to the deck, which the magician shuffles.

a) She then throws the deck in the air so that the cards flutter down around her.

b) As they clear, a single card is seen to be sitting on the back of her still outstretched hand, and this proves to be the card that was taught.

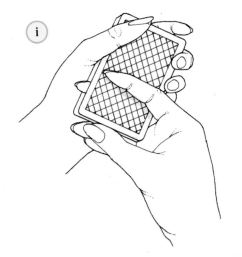

Method: While the volunteer and his friends are drawing the attention of the rest of the audience, you touch the back of your right hand to a blob of something sticky (honey) that you put on your table beforehand. As soon as the card is returned to the deck, make the Pass (see pages 18–19) to bring it to the top. During the process of turning

to throw the cards upward, find the opportunity to press the sticky back of your hand to the back of the chosen card. With your hand turned so that its back is away from the spectators, throw the rest of the deck in the air. In the confusion of the falling cards, simply turn your hand to reveal the card.

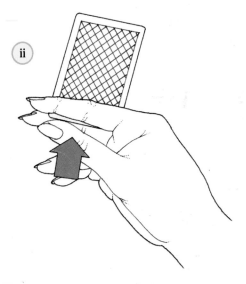

TIP

If you turn your hand too soon or too late, the audience will see what is going on. Because of the stickiness, you should either make this the last trick of your routine or switch decks before the next trick.

It is possible to forgo the use of the honey. **i)** After you have Passed the card to the top of the deck, secure it between your first and second fingers. **ii)** Very quickly move to throw the cards up, simultaneously using your thumb to push the selected card back between the fingers, so that it protrudes to the rear of your hand. Then, as the cards fall all around your outstretched hand, make a lunge with it (as if trying to catch something) and turn it so that the card is revealed.

♠ JACKS WILD

Effect: The magician asks a volunteer to pull out the four Jacks from a full deck, and to arrange them in alternating colors – red, black, red, black. Taking the four cards, she counts them to make sure there is no error and then lays them out on her table. She asks the volunteer to pick out two Jacks of the same color – surely a simple enough task – yet he fails.

Method: The trick lies in the apparently simple act of counting the four cards. Normally you would do this by holding the four face-down in (say) the left hand, thumbing (with the right thumb) the top card into the right hand, thumbing the next card onto the top of this one, etc.; this procedure reverses the order of the cards, but obviously does not affect the alternation of colors. This is what you seem to be doing – and indeed it *is* what you do for the first two cards, except that you are holding the cards between the left hand's thumb and fingertips rather than, more conventionally, further back in the hand.

a) As the right thumb moves to take the third card, you slip the two cards in the right hand and place them underneath the two in the left hand.

b) Then thumb away not a single card but the top three from the packet of four. Finally, you thumb the fourth card quite normally from the left hand onto the top of the three-card packet now in the right hand. The result is that the colors of the four Jacks have become paired, rather than alternating. The maneuver will seem clumsy to you at first, but with a little practice you will be able to perform it as swiftly as if you were executing a conventional count.

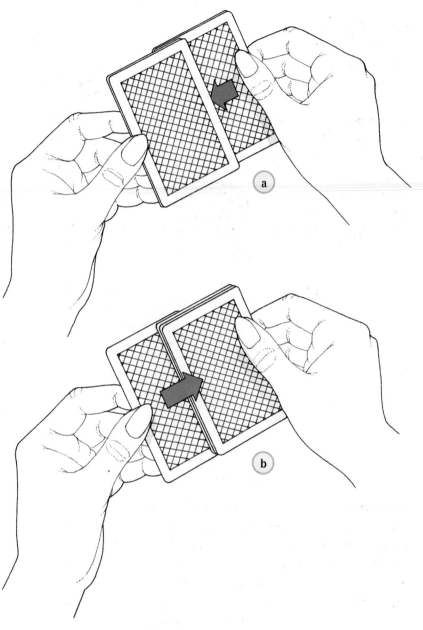

TIP

You can, if you like, draw attention to the count, and thus increase the illusion. When you take the cards, count them normally, keeping them face-up. Whether or not the volunteer shows any interest in this, josh him: "Oh, you're a bit worried about that, are you?" Repeat the count several times in front of him, still with the cards face-up, beginning with exaggerated slowness and then increasing to normal speed. Your point amply demonstrated – that the colors still alternate – you are halfway through the final count as you begin to turn toward your table; it is this final count, of course, that is the false one.

◆ Topsy-Turvy Gamble

Effect: The magician announces that she had one drink too many before the performance and, buoyed by the Dutch courage this has given her, is going to bet a volunteer about the value of a card selected purely at random from a jumbled deck. Stressing that she has only one chance in 52 of getting the right answer, she says that she is willing to bet a world cruise against his watch that she will win. When the volunteer looks dubious about the safety of his watch, she increases the difference: a world cruise with the starlet of his choice against any old scrap of paper he can find in his pocket. The stakes settled, she asks him to shuffle the cards, takes the deck back from him.

a) Saying that she will jumble not only the order of the cards but even the way they are facing, she pulls off a packet from the deck, turns it over and replaces it face-up on the deck.

b) She repeats this with another, larger, packet.

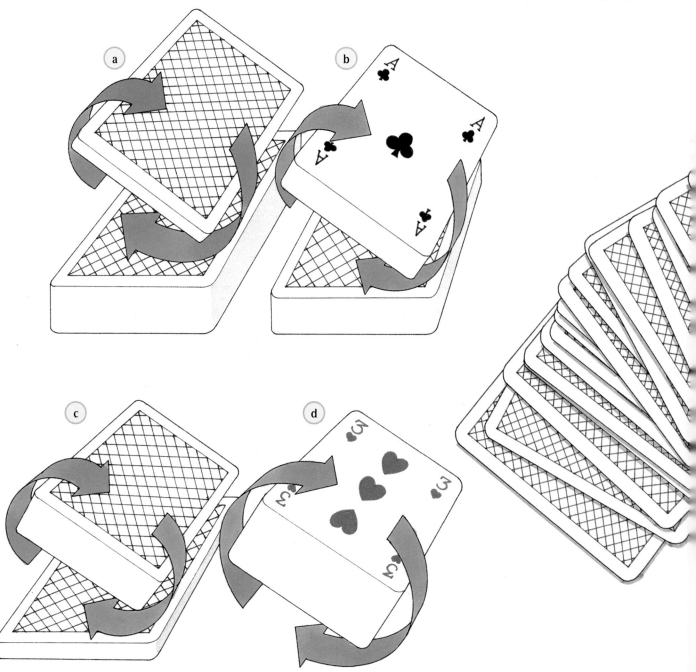

c) Then with another, yet larger.

d) Finally she turns the whole deck over so that everything will be well and truly muddled.

e) She announces that her card is (say) the Two of Clubs, and it will be the first face-down card she comes to as she fans through the deck. Sure enough, that card proves to be the Two of Clubs.

Method: The card on which you are betting is the top card of the deck before the start of the manipulation. The best way to determine which that is is to glimpse the bottom card of the deck as the volunteer gives the cards back to you after shuffling, then swiftly use the Pass (see pages 18–19) to take that card to the top. Thereafter, the net effect of your manipulation – which is nowhere near as jumbling as it looks – is merely to ensure that the deck's initial top card will indeed prove to be the first face-down card exposed as you fan out the deck.

TIP

Practice the manipulation until you can do it naturally, without having to pause and count how many times you have flipped packets over. Bearing in mind the size of the stakes involved, it is a **very good idea** to make sure you have *not* in fact had one drink too many before the performance!

♣ CARDS THAT SPELL (1)

Effect: The magician asks a volunteer to select a card at random from the deck, explaining that she has succeeded in teaching the cards in this particular deck how to spell – well, at least their own names. On the card being returned to the deck, she shuffles and then asks the volunteer to count down from the top of the deck, peeling off one card for each letter of the card he chooses – e.g., T-H-R-E-E-O-F-C-L-U-B-S. At the end of this exercise, it is found to the magician's dismay that the card turned up is not in fact the Three of Clubs. Explaining angrily that cards are, well, a bit thick, she puts the discarded heap back on the deck and shouts at the deck as a whole. This time, when the volunteer spells out his card, it shows as the final "s" of "Clubs".

Method: Have a volunteer pick a card. Using the Pass (see pages 18–19) in the normal way, bring the card to the top of the deck. From here on the trick works itself. Obviously the spelling exercise will produce the wrong card first time around; equally obviously, because the chosen card is at the bottom of the packet you return to the top of the deck, the second attempt will be successful.

♦ CARDS THAT SPELL (2)

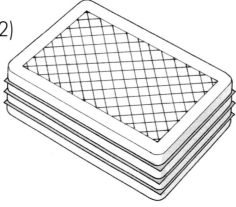

Effect: The magician announces that she has taught the cards in the deck to spell their own names. She asks a volunteer to draw a card from the deck, to tell her what it is, to return it, and to shuffle the deck as much as he wishes; she then explains that, if she spells the name of the card down from the top of the deck, removing one card for each letter of the chosen card's name – e.g., T-H-R-E-E-O-F-C-L-U-B-S – the final card turned up will indeed be the Three of Clubs. To show that there is no deception, she will perform the exercise blindfold – indeed, to make doubly sure, she will even put the deck in her pocket and count from there. Blindfolded, she spells out the cards from the pocket and the final "s" does indeed correspond to the Three of Clubs.

Method: Beforehand, secrete a duplicate deck in your pocket, sorted into suit and rank order; furthermore, divide the suits off from each other with pieces of card just a little bigger than the cards. Put the displayed deck in your pocket while you are asking a volunteer to blindfold you, to make sure the blindfold is secure, etc.; during this time it will seem quite natural that your hand remains in the pocket, and the physical activity of the blindfolding will disguise any movement your arm makes as you pick out the correct card from the duplicate deck. You then spell out random cards from the "real" deck through T-H-R-E-E-O-F-C-L-U-B and produce the duplicate Three of Clubs itself for the final "s".

♥ CARDS THAT SPELL (3)

Effect: The magician sorts out all the cards of one suit (e.g., Spades) from the deck, and puts the rest of the cards to one side. She then explains that the Spades are the cleverest of the suits, and that each of them can spell its own name. She starts spelling them off from the top of the packet with A-C-E, putting each of the first two cards to the bottom of the packet and turning up the Ace to correspond to the "e". Putting the Ace to one side, she continues to spell T-W-O, and the Two is turned up with the "o", and discarded. She continues right through until the final card left in her hands is the King.

Method: As you are sorting out the Spades from the rest, scatter them fairly widely over your table. This will make it less obvious that you are not picking them up again at random but in this order: Queen, Four, Ace, Eight, King, Two, Seven, Five, Ten, Jack, Three, Six, Nine (so that, finally, the Queen is at the top of your face-down packet, the Nine at the bottom). Thereafter, the trick works itself.

> **TIP**
>
> While picking up the Spades, it is a good idea to talk with the audience about the practical difficulties involved in teaching cards their names, or to indulge in some byplay with the audience — anything to disguise the fact that the order in which you are picking up the Spades is other than random. You can invent a mnemonic to help you remember the required order, but this can lead to confusion (two cards begin with "f", two with "s" and three with "t") so your best plan is probably just to learn the order — it doesn't take long.

♠ CARDS THAT SPELL (4)

Effect: The magician asks a volunteer to shuffle the deck and deal out the cards into two equal packets; one for each of them. From his own packet he then selects a card and gives it to the magician, who puts it on top of her packet, followed by the rest of the volunteer's. The magician cuts the deck twice while asking the volunteer to name his card (e.g., the Three of Clubs). The magician then spells out the sentence Y-O-U-R C-A-R-D W-A-S T-H-E T-H-R-E-E-O-F-C-L-U-B-S, turning up a card for each letter. The card turned up at the final "s" of the sentence is indeed the Three of Clubs.

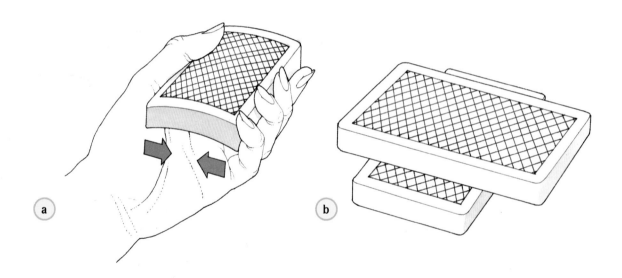

a
b

Method: a) While the volunteer is choosing his card, squeeze the packet in your hand so that the 26 cards in it all gain a slight curve; this will be enough for you to keep this packet separate from the cards returned to you by the volunteer.

b) Once he has done so, it is easy enough to cut the deck first so that the chosen card goes to the bottom of the deck, and second so that the deck is returned to its original order, with the chosen card in the 26th position down from the top. The name of any card in the deck is spelled using between 10 and 15 letters, so all you must do is choose the first part of the sentence according to the numerical value of the card's name. "Three of Clubs" has 12 letters, as do "Four of Hearts",

"King of Spades", etc., so their names require a 14-letter prefix – e.g., "Your card was the". A 15-letter name (e.g., "Seven of Diamonds") needs an 11-letter prefix (e.g., "You chose the"), a 14-letter name (e.g., "Jack of Diamonds") a 12-letter prefix (e.g., "The card is the"), a 13-letter name (e.g., "Queen of Spades") a 13-letter prefix (e.g., "Your card is the"), an 11-letter name (e.g., "Ace of Hearts") a 15-letter prefix (e.g., "You picked out the") and a 10-letter name (e.g., "Six of Clubs") a 16-letter prefix (e.g., "Here's your card, the"). To avoid calculating the number of letters in a card's name each time from scratch, memorize that "of Diamonds" has 10 letters, "of Hearts" and "of Spades" each has 8, and that "of Clubs" has 7.

◆ SWITCHEROO

Effect: The magician asks a volunteer to select two cards and memorize them without showing them to the magician, who is busily shuffling the deck. At any point the volunteer can ask the magician to stop the shuffle, so that he may reinsert the first of his cards; the same applies as he reinserts the second. The magician keeps on shuffling a while longer, to make absolutely sure the cards are randomized. Without pause, the magician lays out the whole deck face-down in a fan on her table, and the first card is shown to be face-up. She pulls it away from the others, shuffles the rest again, reinserts the first card, shuffles a while longer, and then again suddenly spreads out all the cards face-down to reveal the volunteer's second card lying face-up among the rest.

Method: This trick relies on two things: the first is forcing two cards (see pages 20–22).

a) The second is the advance preparation of a double-faced card, by gluing together, back to back, two cards from another deck. If the two faces on the dummy card are (say) the King of Spades and the Ace of Diamonds, all you must do in advance is ensure that, at the outset, the real King and real Ace are placed appropriately for the force used.

b) The double-faced card should start near the bottom of the deck (e.g., at second-bottom), both to ensure that the volunteer does not cut at it and so that you know where it is. Your shuffling can be as thorough as you like, so long as you retain the double-faced card somewhere in the middle of the deck. The first revelation obviously works itself. After that, gather the rest of the cards in your hand face-up, reinsert the double-faced card in the middle of the deck, likewise "face-up", and shuffle for long enough to make it seem that the shuffling is in any way important. When you spread the cards again, the second face shows.

TIP
The easiest way of making sure the deck is set up right is to prepare a deck specially in advance. You can then use this trick as the start of your routine, covertly jettisoning the double-faced card when the trick is over. Alternatively, you can make this the last trick: have the double-faced card plus a duplicate of both King and Ace in a pocket, find some pretext for popping the deck in your pocket for a moment, and withdraw it with the extra cards.

♣ Hop from the Hat

Effect: The magician, talking about how she has always had a head for cards, asks a volunteer to select a card, examine it, and return it to the deck. She places the deck in a borrowed hat. She then flicks the bottom of the hat and the selected card hops up into the air.

a

b

Method: The hat must be a trilby, or any variety of cloth hat with a crease along its crown dividing the interior into two sections. Use any technique to identify the selected card and employ the Pass (see pages 18–19) to bring it to the top of the deck.

a) As you drop the deck into the hat, ensure that the chosen card goes into one section while the bulk of the deck goes into the other.

b) Then simply flick or slap the appropriate section from beneath, and the single card will hop out.

TIP

Ideally the trick should be done with a hat borrowed from a member of the audience, as indicated, so that all possibilities of fakery are plainly nullified. These days, however, you cannot rely on there being anyone present wearing such a hat, so you should bring one with you. If a friend in the audience will bring it, so much the better — but use someone else's hat, if any, in preference to your friend's.

♥ HOP FROM THE DECK

Effect: The magician asks a volunteer seated in the audience to select a card; it is examined and passed back to the magician, who returns it to the deck. No sooner has she gone back to her table, however, than the card jumps out of the deck. Shrugging, she returns to the audience and asks another volunteer to choose a card. Again the same thing happens . . . and again, as often as she wishes. Finally she says crossly: "This deck is just a bit too lively today – it must be all the excitement!" She discards the deck in favor of another for the next trick.

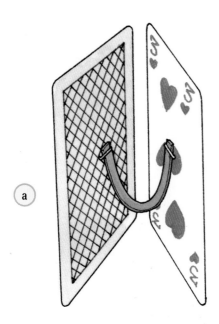

Method: This trick involves gimmicked cards, which is why you must put aside the deck at the end of the trick.

a) Take two cards and between their centers staple or superglue (be careful!) a short piece of elastic – you will have to experiment until you find the right length: short enough that the inserted cards will jump, yet not so short that their edges are damaged when pushed against it. The pair of gimmicked cards should be placed about two-thirds or three-quarters of the way to the bottom of the deck, so that you can fan out most of the rest of it for selection without it being too obvious that there is a bunch of cards held together in your left hand. While the chosen card is being examined, casually square up the rest of the deck; it is easy enough to feel the slight gap caused by the elastic.

b) Push the chosen card back into the deck between the two gimmicked cards, and clutch the deck tightly until you want the chosen card to leap out.

43

♠ HOPSCOTCH FROM THE DECK

Effect: The magician goes among the audience and offers the fanned deck to three volunteers, asking each to select a card. As they examine these, she returns to the front of the audience, shuffling. As the cards are passed back to her, she inserts each into the deck and then goes toward her table. Holding up the deck in a fan, face-out to the audience, she asks the volunteers to concentrate on the cards they chose. Slowly, one by one, these rise from the fan, and she passes them back to the volunteers as keepsakes.

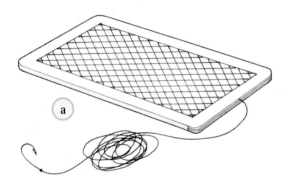

Method: This trick involves a quite elaborate gimmick which is a box, its length and breadth just greater than those of a card and the thickness of six or seven cards; it has a card-face stuck to one side of it and a card-back to the other, and its interior is divided into three partitions – old cards can be used to make the dividers, while the box itself can be constructed of thin card or tin.

a) To the inside of the top center of the box is attached a black thread, at the other end is a sharp hook.

◆ NOT IN THE CLUB

Effect: The magician explains that the suit of Clubs derived its name not from anything to do with weaponry – as might be assumed – or from one of the suits of the Tarot pack – as the more educated would suspect – but from the fact that the cards of that suit are extremely clubbable types: like any old-fashioned gentleman's club, they tend to be strict about the rules of admission, and to blackball "anyone of the wrong suit" who tries to join them. By way of demonstration, she selects the 13 Clubs from a full deck and passes them as one packet and the

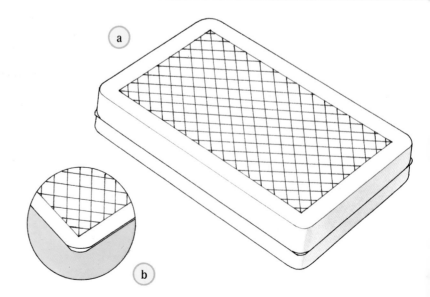

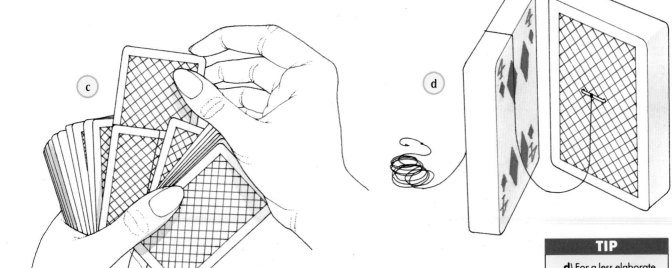

b) When offering the fanned cards, keep the box to the bottom of the deck, shielded by a few bunched cards; have its open end toward you, and keep the deck fairly close to your body, with the thread coiled in your hand. The purpose of the casual shuffle you give the deck as the

volunteers are examining their cards is both to bring the box to the center of the deck and to turn the deck around, so that the opening now faces the audience with the thread running up over the box's aperture and the top of the deck.

c) Push the returned cards into the box in inverse order, if you can, with the first above the second above the third. As you return to your table, with your back to the audience, attach the hook to the front of your costume. Do not fan the deck too broadly as you hold it up to the audience. Slowly extend your arm, and the first card will climb up from the rest. As soon as it is about one-third of the way out, pluck it from position, gather and re-fan the cards, and repeat.

TIP

d) For a less elaborate gimmick using the same principle, staple the end of a thread to the center of a card, which you retain near the bottom of the deck. Proceed much as above, pushing the returned cards into the deck against the thread looped over the ends of the other cards. The advantage of the box is that you make the chosen cards rise from a fanned deck; with the simpler gimmick the deck must be held gathered.
The purpose of giving the chosen cards away as souvenirs is to offer you a pretext for putting the deck to one side, so that you can use a fresh deck for your next trick.

remainder of the deck as another to a volunteer. She asks him to take any card from the rest of the deck and shuffle it into the packet of Clubs. Once he has done so, she asks him to blindfold her (or calls a second volunteer to do this while the first is manipulating the cards) and then to pass her the packet. Immediately she pulls out the intruding card – a feat she can perform again and again.

Method: Beforehand you prepared the Clubs by very gently using fine sandpaper to round down the four corners of the packet.

a) Though the discrepancy will go unnoticed when the cards are in normal use, it will be easy enough to detect any single card in the packet whose corners have *not* been rounded.

b) The amount removed should be very small: sand a tiny amount off the packet first time, find out if that is enough, sand off a tiny amount more if need be, etc.

TIP

Once you have performed the basic trick a couple of times, vary things. Ask the volunteer sometimes to give you an unadulterated packet of Clubs, sometimes to put more than one "intruder" into the packet, without telling you which he is doing.

45
♥

♣ SHOTGUN MARRIAGE

Effect: The magician asks a volunteer to select a card, which proves to be the Queen of Spades. Becoming whimsical, the magician explains how, long after the other three Kings had married their appropriate partners, the King of Spades remained unwed: he had set his heart on the princess of a neighboring land, but her father refused to consent to the marriage. How the two came in the end to be wed, so that she became the Queen of Spades, is not something which the magician wishes to discuss in what is, after all, intended to be a family show. So – on with the trick. She puts the deck face-down on her table and asks the volunteer to cut it anywhere he wants, insert the Queen, and complete the cut. She then fans out the cards, still face-down, and at once it is discovered that one of them – the Jack of Spades – is face-up. Tutting to herself, the magician pulls this card out from the rest,

accidentally pulling also the one beneath it, which she picks up and looks at: it proves to be the King of Spades. This is all, she says, reminding her of the legend of how the King and Queen eventually got married, and she pulls out the next card as well – which is the Queen herself. That was the trouble, the magician remarks darkly as she gathers up the deck in preparation for the next trick: the Jack came first.

Method: a) Beforehand, have the Jack face-up at second-bottom of the deck, the King face-down at the bottom, and the Queen face-down at the top.

b) Shuffle the deck assiduously, but keeping these three cards in their position. Force the Queen on the volunteer using the Riffle Force (see page 21), and then shuffle again, still keeping the Jack and King in their places. The rest of the trick, of course, works itself.

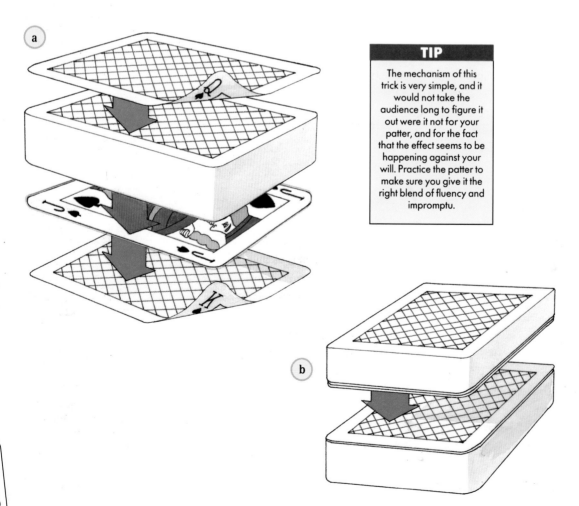

> **TIP**
>
> The mechanism of this trick is very simple, and it would not take the audience long to figure it out were it not for your patter, and for the fact that the effect seems to be happening against your will. Practice the patter to make sure you give it the right blend of fluency and impromptu.

♠ QUICK STUDY

Effect: Boasting idly of her telepathic powers, the magician fans out the cards face-up to a volunteer, cuts them, riffles the deck a few times and then asks him to stop her somewhere mid-riffle and to take the card thus randomly selected; having examined it, he should put it in his pocket. She cuts the deck again, concentrates for a moment, then tells him what his card is.

Method: Although the cards seem to be in random order, the deck is in fact stacked. One simple way of doing this is, first, to have the face-up cards running from the top downward in suit order, with a Spade followed by a Heart followed by a Club followed by a Diamond followed by the next Spade, etc. (Note the alternating colors.) Their numerical value, on the other hand, increases by the count of three each time. The net result of both orderings is that, for example, a sequence within the deck might run Five of Spades, Eight of Hearts, Jack of Clubs, Ace of Diamonds, Four of Spades . . . Cutting the deck does not affect the ordering. Once the volunteer has taken his card, cut the deck at the point where he took the card, and get a glimpse of the new bottom card. This card was the one immediately behind the one he took, so you can quickly work out what card his must have been. For example, if you see the Four of Spades, you know that his card must be the Seven of Hearts, or if you see the Ten of Clubs, you know his card is the King of Diamonds, and so on.

> **TIP**
>
> This is a very easy way of stacking a deck, and can be used in lots of other tricks. But there is no need to stick to this principle: try inventing a few different ways of stacking the deck to gain the same result, and settle on any that might suit you.

♥ SUITS ME

Effect: The magician passes the full deck out to the audience and asks that four volunteers each select a card – the only proviso being that they must confer among themselves to ensure the cards are of different suits. When the deck, sans the four cards, is returned to her the magician rapidly deals it face-up onto her table, and then announces the four missing cards.

Method: This is not a trick: there is no subterfuge at all. What it does require is a lot of practice and a lot of concentration, because you must teach yourself to keep four running totals in your head simultaneously. Imagine that you are keeping four ledger columns, one for each suit, running in the order of superiority used in bridge: Spades, Hearts, Diamonds, Clubs. As you deal each card, add its value (Jack = 11, Queen = 12, King = 13) to the appropriate column. The total for a complete suit is 91, and you can count all the way up if you prefer: a final tally line of 83: 79: 88: 85 means that the missing cards are the Eight of Spades, Queen of Hearts, Three of Diamonds and Six of Clubs. It is easier, however, to learn to count to the base 13, inventing easy names for the extra three digits: 1, 2, 3, 4, 5, 6, 7, 8, 9, x, y, z, 10, 11, 12 . . . Whenever a 10, 11 or 12 appears in a column, forget about the 1, so these become 0, 1, 2. Once the count is complete, simply subtract your answer from 13 to get the value of the missing card.

> **TIP**
>
> This is not an easy art. When learning it at first, try using only 26 cards, the Spades and the Hearts, leaving the others aside. Once you are more confident, start using the Diamonds as well, and then finally add the Clubs. Don't be depressed if it takes a long time to get the knack: in due course you will be able to do it so quickly that you can deal out the cards without any perceptible pause for thought. The technique can be used as part of other tricks – you can always use it to identify a single missing card.

◆ THE SCURVY KNAVES (1)

Effect: Once upon a time, the magician tells her audience, there were not one but four scurvy knaves who stole the Queen of Hearts' tarts. She pulls out the four criminals – i.e., the four Jacks – from the deck to show them to the audience, then places them on top of the deck. The Royal Guards, she explains, chased the knaves until finally they were trapped in a single tower, where they hid. The first of them hid on the ground floor (she puts one Jack at the bottom of the deck), the next hid on the next floor (she puts a Jack in the lower part of the deck), the third near the top of the tower (a Jack in the upper part of the deck) and the fourth was so terrified he shinned right up the flagpole (the final Jack remains at the deck's top). When the Guards came charging in at the base of the tower the thief at the top was so frightened he jumped from his perch (she removes him from the top of the deck and shows him to the audience), and the others all moved up one place. As the Guards came up through the tower, each of the thieves in turn in desperation climbed the flagpole and jumped off (she peels off the remaining Jacks one by one).

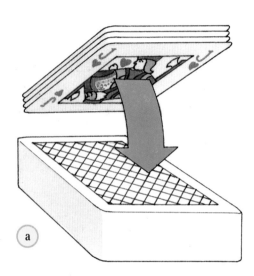

a

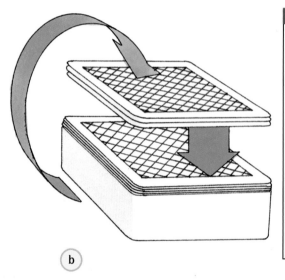

b

TIP

The technique of using three already palmed cards is so well known that it is advisable either to use the Pass (see pages 18–19) or, by contrast, to use the Palming technique (see page 17) and then, as the trick ends, to grin, say something like "Of course, every schoolchild knows *that* trick – but the story really did happen, and it happened like *this* . . .", and then proceed to perform either (or even both) of the next two tricks.

Method: a) The trick begins with your placing the Jacks on top of the deck.

b) Swiftly use the Pass (see pages 18–19) three times to bring three random cards from the bottom to cover them.

c) Alternatively, when you are showing the four Jacks to the audience, already have three palmed cards behind them. Either way, the trick then works itself.

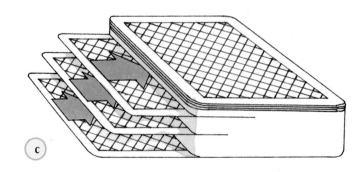

c

♣ THE SCURVY KNAVES (2)

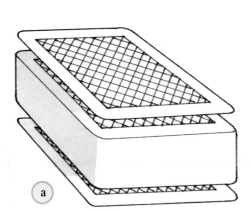

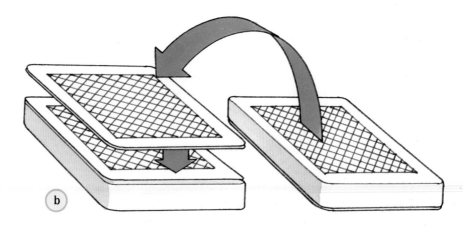

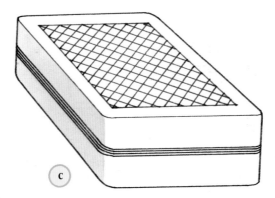

Effect: The magician tells the tale of the Queen of Hearts' tarts, and of how the Royal Guards chased the thieves until they were cornered in one of the Palace towers.

a) As in the previous trick, she explains how one of the criminals fled all the way up the flagpole at the top of the tower, and here she shows the first Jack quite openly to the audience as she places it on the top of the deck. The second thief stayed on the ground floor: she displays the next Jack as a single card and quite openly places it at the bottom of the deck.

b) Putting down the deck on the table in front of her and cutting it, she tells how the remaining two Jacks – both red or both black – were brothers, as can be seen by their colors. They stuck together and, worried equally by the prospects of Royal Paratroopers from above and Royal Tunnelers from below, ended up rather indecisively clutching each other for comfort halfway up the tower: she places them in the middle of the deck, which she now picks up.

c) In fact, the brothers were right to worry: the various divisions of Guards drove one thief down from the flagpole and another up from the basement, so that all four were in the middle of

the tower when finally arrested – as the magician demonstrates by splaying out the deck to show all four Jacks at its center.

Method: The cut is the phony, and it is important that your patter is sufficiently involved and entertaining that no one thinks too much about it. When you cut the cards, make sure you know which packet is which. You put the two "brothers" into the center of the deck by placing them on top of what was the *upper* packet, and then place the other packet on top of that. This automatically brings together the four Jacks in the middle of the deck.

TIP

As noted, your patter is extremely important if the audience is to be distracted from the very simple cheat you are performing. You might like to plant an accomplice in the audience to further distract attention: she can be a rowdy, difficult customer, constantly yelling that she knows this trick and accusing you of performing the preceding trick – i.e., The Scurvy Knaves (1). Her gibes and your demonstrations of innocence (no palmed cards, etc.) should create enough diversion for the real mechanism to go unnoticed.

If the deception is detected, laugh it off and say you were just performing another demonstration of a well known trick: the thieves in fact fled not to a tower but to the Royal Gardens ... and segue into The Scurvy Knaves (3).

49

♥

♥ THE SCURVY KNAVES (3)

Effect: Once upon a time, says the magician, four scurvy knaves stole the Queen of Hearts' tarts (she shows the Jacks and returns them to the top of the deck) and fled from her wrath, being chased by the Royal Guards into the Palace Gardens, of which there were four. Each thief chose a different garden (the magician deals out the four Jacks face-down and separately), and they hid themselves by pulling bushes over them (she deals three cards onto the top of each Jack).

She then moves the four heaps around, to further confuse the pursuers. She now calls upon the audience to take the part of the Royal Guards, and to yell out a number between one and four to decide which garden to look in. Picking up the cards of the appropriate heap, she tells how the four thieves were eventually discovered cowering together in a single garden – and, sure enough, the pile is discovered to consist only of the four Jacks.

♠ JOKER'S DELIGHT

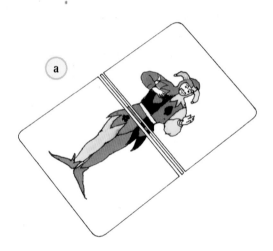

Effect: With a volunteer by her side, the magician holds up three cards – two nondescript cards with a Joker between them. She announces that the volunteer is going to play Find the Joker – just like Find the Lady – with the audience. Asking them to watch the cards carefully, she turns them face-down and very deliberately sets them out on the table in front of her. She tells the volunteer to move the cards around, but of course to keep his own eyes on the Joker so that he will know what he is doing. She lets him accept a couple of unsuccessful calls from the audience, then asks him to turn up the Joker himself. It proves that the Joker has disappeared entirely, leaving a nondescript card in its place.

Method: As soon as the four Jacks have been shown and returned to the top of the deck, use the Pass (see pages 18–19) repeatedly to place three cards on top of them. The fourth card you deal will thus be the first Jack. Make something of a palaver about the way the thieves pulled the bushes over themselves as you count out three cards onto each pile, so that the audience do not think too much about the fact that you are putting "bushes" on the fourth Jack first (in fact it is the other three Jacks you are putting on top of him), the "third Jack" second, and so on. Your purpose in moving the heaps around is to ensure that the four Jacks end up in one of the two middle positions. When you ask the audience to yell out numbers between one and four, a good contingent will certainly call for either two or three; you count the heaps in the appropriate direction (left to right or right to left) to settle on the one containing four Jacks.

Method: a) Beforehand, cut out a thin central section from a Joker and throw it away, leaving yourself with the card's top and bottom.

b) Using clear tape, fix the edge of the top part of the Joker to the back of the edge of the lower part; turn it round so that the sticky tape is on the inside of the fold.

c) You can now hang the assemblage over the top of another card, with part of the Joker showing to the front over the card's own face.

d) When you present the three cards they are one above the other, gripped at the sides, with the dummied card in the middle so that it looks like a Joker; your grip is backhand – i.e., using the left hand, your thumb is to the left of the packet.

e) To deal out the cards, bring the hand down so that its back is upward in front of you. Tap the card edges quickly on your table to shove what was the uppermost card through your hand and level with the rest.

f) Then (with the hand again back-upward) pull the cards one by one from your hand to lay them on the table, leaving the assemblage in your hand. Get rid of it as soon as possible while the volunteer is diverting the audience by moving the cards around.

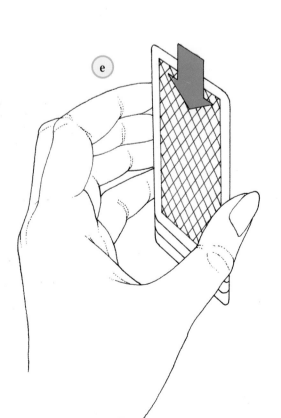

e

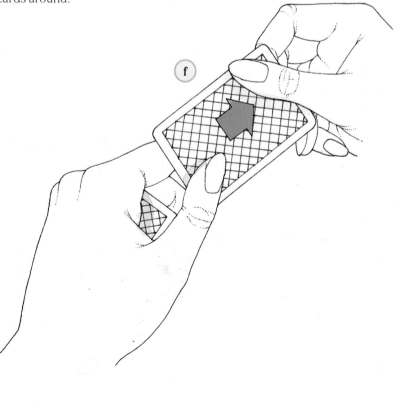

f

◆ DOUBLEBACK

Effect: The magician writes a prediction on a sheet of paper, which she folds and tucks into a volunteer's pocket. She then offers him a full deck of cards, fanned out face-up, and asks him to pick a card (e.g., the King of Hearts), quite openly. The magician puts the King back on top of the deck; then immediately lifts it up to show the audience that its back is of a different design to that of all the other cards in the deck (red when it should be blue, or any other similar clash), which she fans out by way of demonstration. Putting the deck to one side, she explains that the King came from her other deck (with appropriately designed

backs), which she now picks up, adding the King to it, and shuffles once or twice while asking the volunteer to read out the prediction that she put in his pocket earlier: "You will pick the card with the wrong back – *twice*!" While he is still reading she fans out the second deck, face-out to the audience, showing that it, too, has an odd card. She draws this card and turns it to show the audience that it is the King of Hearts. But this deck was lying out of reach while the volunteer was making his selection – so how could she have known which would be the right card to substitute between the two decks?

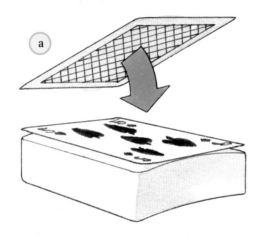

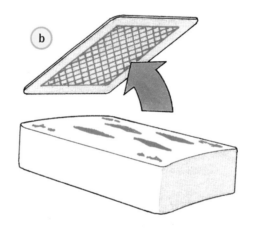

Method: Imagine you start with a blue-backed deck. Remove one card from it – any card (e.g., the Five of Spades) – and don't even bring this card onstage with you. Crimp all the remaining blue-backed cards so that they have a slight warp upward (when face-up). Substitute the missing card with the same one from (e.g.) a red-backed deck, and keep this card at the bottom of the deck as you shuffle prior to the trick's start. Keeping the deck face-up, have the volunteer pick any card (e.g., the King of Hearts). As he pulls it out of the fan, close up the fan.

a) With everything still face-up, put the King on top of the deck – in fact, on top of your uncrimped Five.

b) Because of the crimping, it is easy immediately to pick off these two cards together to show that the King apparently has a red back. Add the two cards to the red-backed deck, shuffle briefly, and at any time you can now show that the King of Hearts in *this* deck is the only one with a *blue* back.

♣ DOUBLECROSS

Effect: Explaining that she is about to conduct an experiment in "subliminal telepathy", the magician asks for two volunteers, one to stand at either side of the stage. She blindfolds each of them in turn. Picking up a deck of cards, she shuffles it, fans it briefly both face-out and back out at the audience to show that it is perfectly normal, then gives each of the blindfolded volunteers a broad-tipped red marker pen. After giving the second pen, she crosses the stage, still shuffling, and fans the cards in front of the first volunteer, asking him to pick one with his fingers, draw it out, and mark its face with a big cross. After he has done so, she lets him put the card back in the deck by "feel". She repeats all this with the second volunteer, but asking him to mark the *back* of his chosen card. Giving the cards a final shuffle, she moves to stage center and asks the volunteers to remove their blindfolds. She fans the cards face-up and asks

the first to identify his card by the cross: it is (say) the Two of Diamonds. Leaving the card in place, she fans the deck face-down to the second volunteer, asking him to find his card by the cross. When he pulls it out it proves to be the Two of Diamonds! So subliminal was the telepathy operating between the two volunteers, explains the magician, that neither of them knew it was happening – yet they both picked the same card!

Method: The trick is embarrassingly simple. You have already marked both front and back of the Two of Diamonds with a big red cross; so that the audience is not aware of this, the card is next to your hand as you fan the deck at the trick's start, and thereafter you shuffle it to the center. The two marker pens you give to the volunteers share one thing in common – they don't work, because you took the precaution of drying them out beforehand!

♥ X-RAY FINGERS

Effect: The magician shuffles the deck and asks a volunteer to cut it. For this trick, she announces, she needs to get rid of two cards, because she will be wanting to deal out five equal heaps. She asks him to remove a couple of the cards – two which have always been regarded as unlucky: the Ace and Queen of Spades. As he removes each, first the Ace and then the Queen, he should cut the deck at that point and complete the cut. After both have been removed, she asks him to deal out the remaining 50 cards into five face-down heaps. Pressing her fingertips to the top of the first heap, she screws up her eyes in concentration and then announces that the top card is (say) the Jack of Hearts – which sure enough it proves to be. She repeats the process with the remaining four heaps, each time correctly identifying the top card.

Method: Before the trick starts, you stack the bottom of the deck with five cards whose values and order you have memorized, plus, at the very bottom, the Queen of Spades. As you shuffle, keep these cards together at the bottom. The volunteer's cuts make no difference to this ordering, but his completed cut when removing the Queen has the effect of bringing the five memorized cards once more to the bottom of the deck. These five cards are, of course, the ones that will be dealt out last, and so will be on top of the five heaps.

♠ Swap (1)

Effect: The magician shuffles the deck thoroughly and then gives half of it to a volunteer. She asks him to spread the cards of his packet out on the table and to draw a single card from the middle somewhere; she will do the same with her own half. She announces her chosen card as (say) the Jack of Clubs and asks him to tell his – e.g., the Seven of Spades. Both then put their cards on top of their own packets, gather the packets and cut them, so that the two cards are in the centres of their respective packets. The magician then proposes they both fan out their packets for a final look at the cards they drew to see that all is well. To his astonishment, the

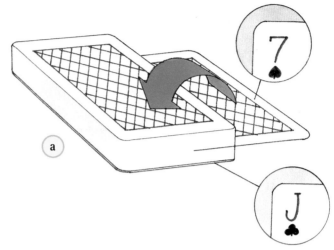

volunteer discovers that the Jack of Clubs has migrated to his packet, and is now nestling right beside his own Seven of Spades.

♦ Swap (2)

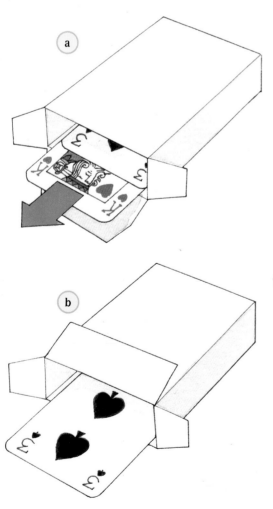

Effect: The magician asks a volunteer to select two cards – e.g., the Three of Spades and the King of Hearts – and show them to the audience. She gives him an end-opening box (a card-box is fine) and asks him to put both cards into it. She tells the company that she knows what intelligent and observant people they are, and how nervous she is performing in front of such a discerning crowd – they will have no trouble in keeping track of just two cards, will they?

a) So saying, she takes back the box, pulls one card (e.g., the King of Hearts) out of it, and places that card face-down on her table. Obviously the card left in the box will be the Three of Spades; there's no need, she blusters, to check. The audience naturally makes sounds of discontent, so she eventually tells the volunteer to take a look: sure enough, the Three is still in the box. Picking up the King of Hearts and showing it, she returns it to the box, and this time pulls out the Three of Spades, which she displays ostentatiously as she returns to her table. Again, she says, there is no need to check the contents of the box . . . again she eventually tells the volunteer to do so.

b) He finds the Three of Spades there, and the magician, looking surprised, turns up the card on her table to show it has become the King of Hearts.

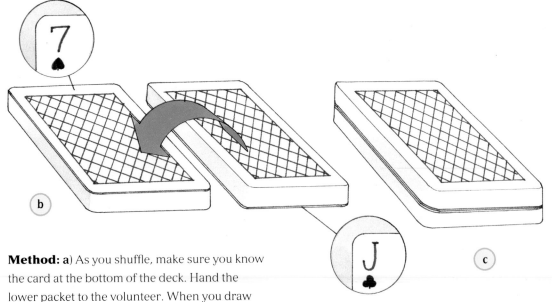

Method: a) As you shuffle, make sure you know the card at the bottom of the deck. Hand the lower packet to the volunteer. When you draw out the card from your own spread packet, announce it as the Jack of Clubs – whatever its true value might be.

b) The volunteer makes the cut.

c) In doing so, he places his own card next to the Jack.

> **TIP**
>
> Although it is always easier to ascertain the value of the card at the bottom of the deck, it is easier to retain the top card in its position while performing the shuffle; moreover, there is a possibility that the volunteer may inadvertently notice the bottom card of the packet you hand him. Better, therefore, that the Jack of Clubs be at the top of the deck. If you like, you can give the cards a genuine shuffle, glimpse the bottom card, and then make the Pass (see pages 18–19) to take it to the top.

Method: c) The gimmick is a double-sided card, which you can make by very carefully pasting back-to-back the Three of Spades and King of Hearts from an old deck; use a warm iron to make the fake as thin as possible. (You can buy printed double-sided cards, but they rarely look convincing.) Force the two cards on the volunteer using the Riffle Force or Cut it Yourself (see page 21); the dummy is already lying on your table, with the King face-down. When you pick up the King to "return" it to the box, pick up the dummy instead. Take the box from the volunteer so that you can put the dummy into it, pull out the Three and put both cards in together. Start to give the box back to the volunteer but change your mind halfway.

d) This action allows you to turn the box over.

e) Pull the dummy out again, this time displaying the Three of Spades side as you go to your table. At the final revelation, simply pick up the real King of Hearts, so that both cards and the box can safely be examined by the audience.

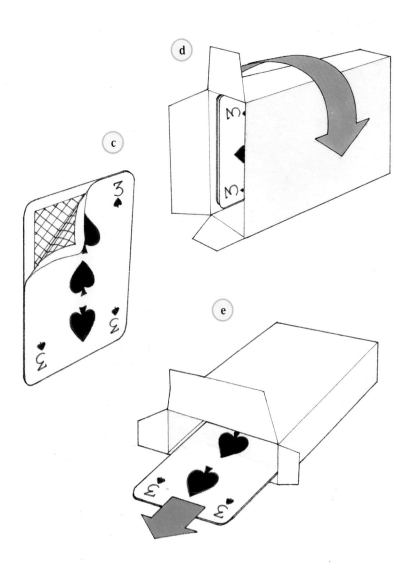

> **TIP**
>
> When picking up the dummy from your table you are also, so far as the audience is concerned, turning up a card that you laid there face-down. To turn up the correct face of the dummy, take it by the edge closer to the audience and lift – otherwise you risk giving a glimpse of the wrong side.

♣ Reciting the Deck (1)

Effect: The magician passes out a deck of cards so that a volunteer from the audience can shuffle it. As it is being passed back to her, she notices that another member of the audience looks dissatisfied, so she insists that he shuffle it as well. Still muttering about cynics and directing angry glares and insults at him, she returns the deck to her table, and proceeds to turn up the cards one by one, calling out each one before she turns it up. To general amazement – not least that of the skeptical audience member, whom she is still insulting – she is right every time.

Method: The "cynic" can be any member of the audience: there is bound to be someone whom you can at least pretend to see looking dubious. The point of picking on someone like this is to distract attention toward him – and away from the fact that you are swapping the shuffled deck for a prepared one. This deck you have ordered as follows: Ace of Clubs, Eight of Diamonds, Five of Hearts, Four of Spades, Jack of Clubs . . . This order seems random to the audience, but in fact it is not. What you have done is set the cards in two alphabetical orders at once: Clubs, Diamonds, Hearts, Spades and Ace, Eight, Five, Four, Jack, King, Nine, Queen, Seven, Six, Ten, Three, Two.

> **TIP**
>
> It is very unlikely that the audience will notice the regularity of the ordering. However, if you are worried about it, run the order of suits backward and forward: Clubs, Diamonds, Hearts, Spades, Spades, Hearts, Diamonds, Clubs, Clubs . . . Or you can vary things by having two Clubs in a row followed by a Diamond, a Heart, and a Spade; then a Club, two Diamonds, a Heart and a Spade: then a Club, a Diamond, two Hearts and a Spade; and so on.

♥ RECITING THE DECK (2)

Effect: As in the previous trick, the magician passes out the deck to the audience for thorough shuffling. It can be returned directly to her or, as before, there can be a diversion as she accuses a member of the audience of excessive skepticism – if he demurs, she tells him that she has X-ray eyes and can see the thoughts bubbling through his brain, whatever the expression on his face might be saying. Once she has the deck again, she puts it behind her back for a final shuffle, then casually shows both sides of it to the audience as she holds it up in front of her. Again (or for the first time) talking about her X-ray eyes, she proceeds to call out the name of each card correctly before pulling it from the back of the deck and throwing it (see page 32) to the audience for verification.

Method: When you put the deck behind your back you do not in fact shuffle it. That is a lie to account for the movements of your arms as you do two things.

a) Reverse the card at the top of the deck so that it is not face-down but face-up; and draw from a pocket or other place of concealment a card (perhaps the Joker) of the same or an identical deck, from which you have torn off the top left-hand corner and which you place face-down on the bottom of the deck. As you bring the deck back into the view of the audience, make sure you have your thumb over the torn-away corner.

b) With the dummy face-up card toward the audience, you can now see the top corner of each card facing you and can read its value. Do make a point of throwing each card to the audience for checking; that way the spectators' attention will be drawn away from the fact that the cards are facing the wrong way as you pull them from the deck.

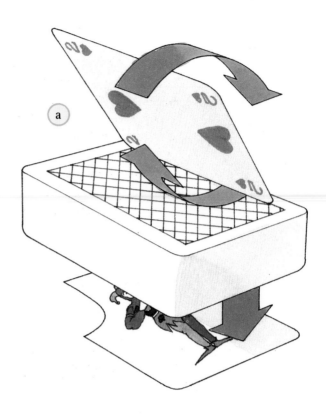

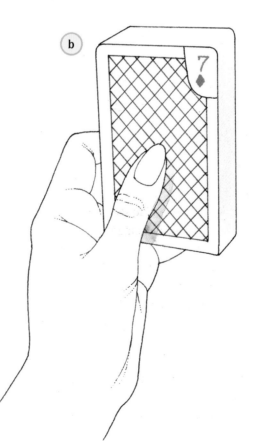

> **TIP**
>
> An alternative is to glimpse the corner of the card as you first bring the deck out from behind your back, then put the deck again behind your back, move the observed card around so that it is the new face-out card, then announce that card as you bring the deck up in front of you. Repeat as many times as you wish. This technique is obviously more cumbersome, but has the advantage that you can then perform the trick blindfold – assuming the blindfold has been put in place by an accomplice so that you can squint down your nose to see the revealed corner as you take the deck behind you.

♠ CLEMENTINE'S CARD TRICK

Effect: The magician tells the audience this trick was invented in 1849 by none other than the father of Darling Clementine, who later taught it to his daughter, who in turn taught it to her Little Sister, who finally passed it on to Stephen Foster as the only way she knew to get his hands off her. The authenticity of this tale – which the audience may not completely believe at first – can be gauged from the fact that it uses only 49 cards, rather than the complete deck: this was because Clementine's father lost three cards from his deck during all the hurly-burly of the Gold Rush, hence the expression "49er" – a fascinatingly convincing little item of historical verisimilitude. Discarding three cards, the magician gives the rest to a volunteer and asks him to select one mentally, shuffle the deck, turn it face-down and then deal the cards into seven face-up heaps. Standing well away ("This was the bit the Little Sister appreciated most"), she asks him to check through the heaps until he finds the one containing his card. She then asks for the number of that heap (counting left to right) and asks him to pile up the heaps by putting the second on top of the first, the third on top of both of them, the fourth on top of that, etc., then to deal the reassembled face-down deck once more into seven face-up heaps and again to report which heap contains his card. The magician tells the audience that the Little Sister used to make Stephen Foster repeat this over and over again,

but that twice is enough for the purposes of demonstration. She asks the volunteer to pile up the cards as before and then to start dealing them out again, one by one. After a short while she stops him, and tells him that the next card will be his – which, of course, it is.

Method: The trick basically works itself: all you have to do is a little calculation. From the second reported heap number subtract 1, and then multiply this new number by 7; add the first reported heap number, and the total gives the position of the card in the deck when it is ready for the final deal. For example, imagine that at the outset the volunteer's card is the third one down from the top of the deck. On the first deal, it will clearly be at the rear of heap 3. On the second deal, it shows third from the rear of heap 1. Now $1 - 1 = 0$, and $7 \times 0 = 0$; $0 + 3 = 3$, and sure enough this card will be the third dealt off next time.

> ### TIP
> More usually, the result of your calculation will be a number somewhere in the 20s or 30s, which is a lot of cards to count. In this event (or even if not), don't make anything special of the final deal, but, while the volunteer is laying the cards out as before, start looking impatient and remark to the audience that by this time even the Little Sister was getting bored. At the right moment, stalk across to the table and pull the correct card from its place.

♥ ODDLY EVEN

Effect: The magician spreads out the deck on the table and asks a volunteer to pick up a bunch at random – he should not look at what he is doing, but merely grab a handful. The magician asks him to take away his cards to a corner of the stage to count them, while she herself casually scoops up a handful of cards, but doesn't look at them. She tells the volunteer that, if he has an odd number of cards, she will make it even by adding her own packet; conversely, if he has an even

number of cards, she will make it odd. She asks him to tell the audience whether the number he counted was even or odd, and then passes her packet to him and asks him to count the cards again: sure enough, the new total is as she originally predicted.

♦ POKER CHAMP

Effect: The magician announces gravely that she is going to tell the story of how her great-grandfather met his death. He was playing poker in the Te Deum Club with three friends (she deals out four hands from the top of the deck) and he easily won the first hand. She turns up her great-grandfather's hand and shows four Sevens; turning it face-down again, she turns up each of the other hands likewise, showing that they have no particularly useful cards. One of her great-grandfather's friends dropped out, she explains (she discards the winning hand and collects up the other three), but the three "survivors" played on (she deals out three hands using the collected cards), and again her great-grandfather won: this time, as she demonstrates, he had four Aces while the other two had nothing useful. Again someone dropped out, leaving just two of them (she discards the winning hand, and deals out two fresh hands from the collected cards). This third time her great-grandfather won was too much for the credulity of the others: she turns up her great-grandfather's hand and shows that now he had a straight five-flush of Spades from Nine through King. He was given, says the magician dolefully, a revolver and told to go off into the library and Do The Decent Thing – *that's* how he met his death.

Method: And so he should have! He had rigged the top 20 cards of the deck (from the top downward) as follows: Ace, Any, King of Spades, Seven, Any, Ace, Any, Seven, Nine of Spades, Any, Ace, Seven, Ace, Queen of Spades, Any, Seven, Ten of Spades, Any, Jack of Spades, Any. This will give the desired effect if you pick up the used hands correctly: each should be placed face-down again after being shown, and for the next deal you should pick up first the hand to your right, place it on top of the hand to its right, etc.

Method: This is an ideal opening trick for a routine to be performed in front of small children – most adults will realize that you merely made sure it had an odd number of cards, since odd + odd = even, and odd + even = odd. (Practice to make sure that you can do this quickly, so that it is not obvious you are counting your handful before you scoop it up.) Even among small children there is a chance that someone will spot the trick. Either way, immediately explain what you have done – this is why this is a good opening trick, because at the end of your explanation you say: "*That* was obvious enough – it really was just a trick: there was no magic involved. The *other* tricks I'm going to perform, however, *do* need magic . . ." And then you proceed to amaze your audience, who will be doubly baffled because they will be trying to find an equally simple mathematical underpinning for tricks that do not rely upon one.

♣ FIND YOUR OWN CARD

Effect: The magician asks a volunteer to select a card, examine it, and return it to the deck. After briefly shuffling, she starts to deal out the cards face-down from the bottom of the face-down deck, asking the volunteer to stop her at any time. When he does so, she deals the next card face-up, and it is of course the chosen card.

a

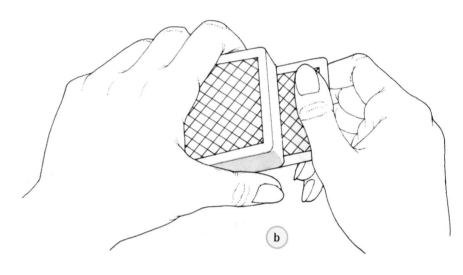

b

Method: The principle of this trick can come in useful in others; it can also be used as a way of forcing cards.

   a) After the card has been returned to the deck, move it to the bottom using whatever technique you prefer.

   b) Hold the deck face-down and tilted slightly toward the volunteer; your grip should be overhand, with your fingers and thumbs wrapping around the deck so that the ends of your fingers make a good friction contact with the bottom card. Slide this card an inch or so back toward your wrist. You can then quite naturally deal out the cards above it one by one until the volunteer calls a halt, at which time you simply ease the chosen card forward and deal it as the next card.

> ### TIP
> You may find it easier to deal the cards "wrong-handed". In other words, if you would normally hold the deck in your left hand and deal the cards with your right, for this you might try holding the deck with your right and dealing with your left. It all depends how strongly "handed" you are to either right or left.

♥ FULL FRONTAL

Effect: The magician asks a volunteer to take a card and then shuffle and cut the rest of the deck thoroughly. She puts this residue of the deck face-down on the palm of her outstretched right hand and asks the volunteer to take the top part of it back from her. The cards of this packet he may again shuffle, if he wishes, before placing them face-down on the palm of her outstretched left hand. On top of this packet he should place his chosen card, and then he should in effect complete the cut by transferring the stack from her right hand onto the top of that in her left. The magician takes the deck and fans the cards face-out toward the audience, then draws the chosen card smoothly from its place in the fan.

Method: As soon as you have passed the deck to the volunteer, palm (see page 17) from your pocket or elsewhere into your right hand a face-down card from a deck with a differently designed back.

a) Take the deck with your left hand and put it face-down on top of the dummy in your right.

b) The volunteer places his card on top of the left-hand packet, while the dummy remains at the bottom of the right-hand packet.

c) The effect of the volunteer's completing the cut is to set the dummy card directly over his chosen one.

d) You can then locate it instantly.

TIP

Of course, you run the risk that the dummy card — e.g., the Three of Spades — may be close to the Three of Spades belonging to the main deck — a coincidence that would make the deception obvious as you fanned the cards. It may even be that the volunteer's chosen card *is* the Three of Spades! You should therefore use both hands when fanning the cards — something that will be natural enough, since you are fanning the full deck and do not wish to drop any. If holding the base of the deck with your right hand, use the fingers of your left at the top of the deck to help fan the cards. Spread the cards quite slowly. As soon as you notice the dummy card emerging from the bunched cards, let a fingertip drop behind the cards to push the dummy in the opposite direction from that in which you are fanning.

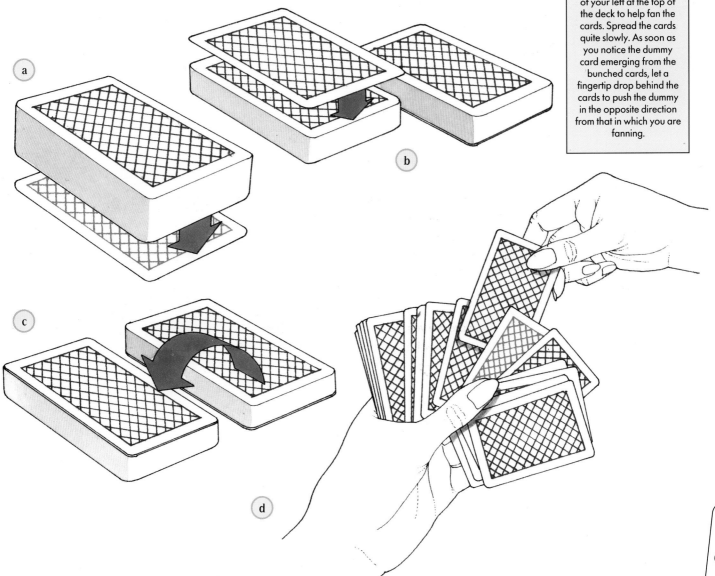

♠ BAD AIM

Effect: The magician explains that she and a friend in the audience have been experimenting for the past few months with telepathy, and have discovered that they can pick up mental messages not only from each other but also, occasionally, from other people – as she will now demonstrate. She introduces her friend to the audience, then sends her to the back of the hall and calls for a volunteer. The volunteer selects a card, notes its value and shows it to one other member of the audience (as umpire) but nobody else, and returns it to the deck. The magician asks him to stand to one side and concentrate very

hard on the card he chose, trying to beam its image to her friend; whatever he is asked, he must simply nod or shake his head. She calls back the friend and spreads out the cards face-up on her table. "Was it," says the magician as she picks up the appropriate card, "the Three of Diamonds?" Immediately the friend claims that it was, and they look to the volunteer . . . who shakes his head. The friend makes a similarly inaccurate positive identification of the next few cards the magician chooses, and the magician grows steadily angrier. Finally she turns to the audience and asks if anyone *else* has a clue. To

♦ HOLEY HANDKERCHIEF

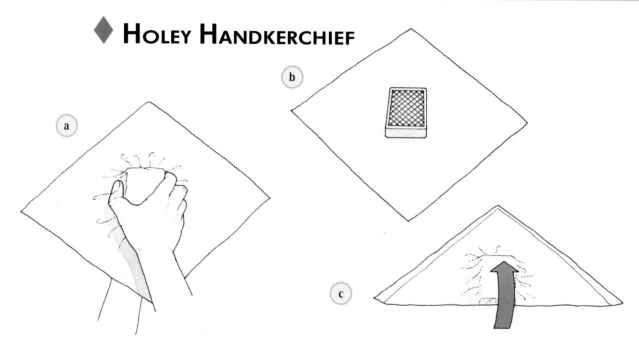

Effect: The magician asks a volunteer to pick a card, which he examines and returns to the deck. She produces a handkerchief, passes it around for examination and drapes it over the deck to demonstrate that it is completely opaque – there is no way that she or anyone else can tell what the cards are through it. She then takes the deck and wraps it in the handkerchief. Holding the package by its "tail", she gives it a few jerks, and suddenly a card drops through the cloth. It proves, of course, to be the chosen card. Handkerchief and deck can then be examined.

Method: As soon as the chosen card has been returned to the deck, execute the Pass (see pages 18–19) to bring it to the top.

  a) Drape the handkerchief (with one corner pointing toward you) over the face-down deck, but as you withdraw the deck with one hand, leave the other hand, still holding the chosen card, under the handkerchief (which really *is* opaque!).

  b) Immediately place the deck face-down on top of the handkerchief, over the chosen card.

  c) Then flip the near corner of the cloth up and over the deck.

everyone's surprise – especially the volunteer's – a hesitant voice from the back suggests (say) the Eight of Spades . . . which proves to be the right card. The magician berates the volunteer for having aimed his telepathic beam in the wrong direction – or maybe it was the fault of the umpire in the audience . . .

Method: You forced the Eight of Spades on the volunteer using one of the techniques described on pages 20–22. For the presentation of the trick you require two accomplices: the friend who always guesses wrong, and the diffident person at the back of the hall. The friend onstage can clown as much as she wishes; the other accomplice has a more subtle part to play, not only acting as just another member of the audience but also, after the trick, explaining to those around her how the image of the Eight of Spades kept appearing in her mind, no matter what else she tried to think of . . .

> ### TIP
> You can have the volunteer and the umpire choose the card between themselves. Either they must tell you the card they choose or you must find a means of glimpsing it. Beforehand, you have arranged with the accomplices that there will be two "clue cards"; e.g., the Queen of Spades and the Seven of Hearts. Both know that the second card you propose after the Queen of Spades will be the correct one. The second "clue card" is a back-up in case the Queen of Spades is the chosen card.

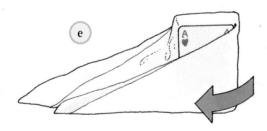

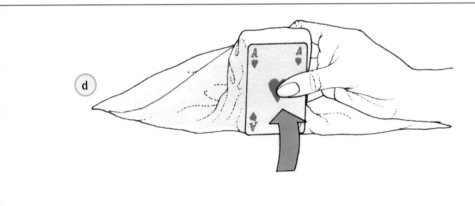

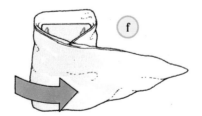

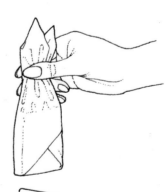

d) With your free hand, grip the deck (through the cloth) and the chosen card and turn the package vertically toward you, so that you can now see the chosen card.

e) Take one of the loose-hanging flaps of handkerchief and fold it toward the other side.

f) Then take both flaps and fold them back again, tugging on the cloth so that the folds hold the chosen card tightly in place.

g) You can now dangle the package by its "tail" reasonably casually until you decide to start jerking it, at which time the chosen card will shake itself free.

> ### TIP
> You can borrow a handkerchief from the audience if you like, but that is always a bit of a gamble – especially if the audience are children! You need the handkerchief to be opaque, clean and large enough, so it is probably best to resist the temptation of gaining added effect by borrowing one.

♣ SIMON SAYS

Effect: The magician reminds the audience of the children's game Simon Says, and says that she would like to play it with a volunteer from the audience. She gives the volunteer one deck of cards and produces another for herself, which she starts to shuffle, bullying him to do the same ("Simon says shuffle the cards"). When she begins using the Hindoo Shuffle (see pages 18–19) he finds himself in difficulties; she apologizes for teasing him ("Simon says sorry"). She then sits down at her table; he does the same. They cut and shuffle the cards a few times and then swap decks. She takes a card from the middle of her new deck and makes a great show of memorizing it, though not saying what it is; he is exhorted to do likewise. She places her card on top of her deck, and cuts it to the middle; he follows suit. They then swap decks again, and each cut their decks a few times. Suddenly, the magician says: "I wonder if you *really* did as Simon said." She turns up her cards and pulls out one of them (e.g., the Jack of Diamonds), showing it to the audience but not to the volunteer: "This is the card that *Simon* chose." He does likewise – and his card, too, is the Jack of Diamonds.

Method: While shuffling your deck, notice that the bottom card is (say) the Ace of Clubs.

a) This is the deck from which the volunteer picks his card; the effect of his cutting is to place that Ace directly over his chosen card.

b) Further cutting does not affect the cards' order, so that, when the deck is returned and you pick it up to "look for the card you chose", it is easy to pick out the volunteer's. He, of course, picks out the *other* Jack of Diamonds.

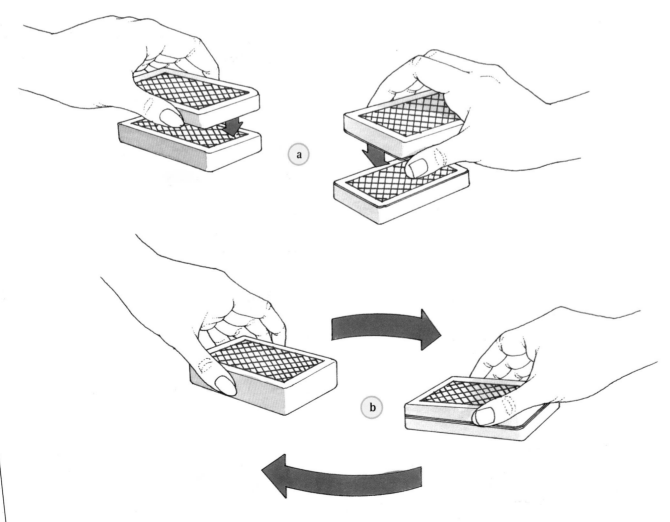

♥ UNFAIR DEAL

Effect: The magician fans the deck, face-down, and asks a volunteer to take any card from it. While he is examining the card, she deals out the rest of the deck face-down into four equal heaps. (Not quite equal! One will be a card short of the other three. But this is irrelevant.) Turning her back, she asks the volunteer to place his card on top of one of the heaps, then to pile the four heaps on top of each other and give the deck back to her. Turning, she instantly fans out the cards on the table and pulls from the fan the volunteer's chosen card.

Method: Beforehand, you set all of the Fives as the top four cards in the deck and all of the Eights as the bottom four. With a little care, you can learn how to apparently shuffle the deck while retaining these cards in their places. Once you've dealt the cards into four equal heaps, each one will have an Eight on the bottom and a Five on top. When you fan out the cards the volunteer's one will be immediately obvious to you – it will be the only card in the deck to lie between a Five and an Eight.

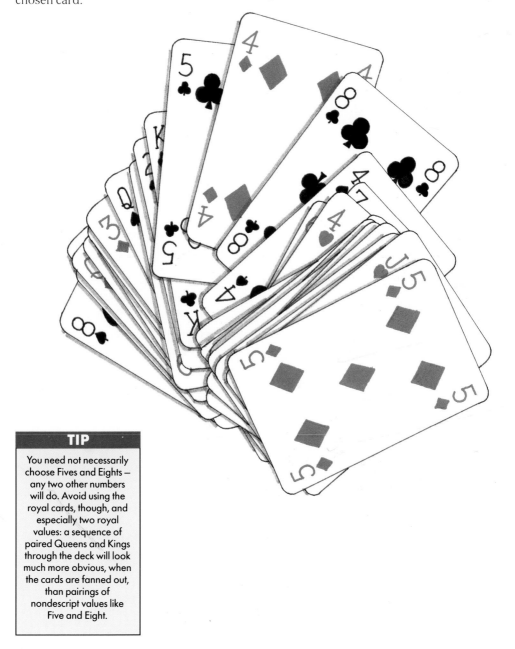

You need not necessarily choose Fives and Eights – any two other numbers will do. Avoid using the royal cards, though, and especially two royal values: a sequence of paired Queens and Kings through the deck will look much more obvious, when the cards are fanned out, than pairings of nondescript values like Five and Eight.

♠ UNEXPECTED THIEF

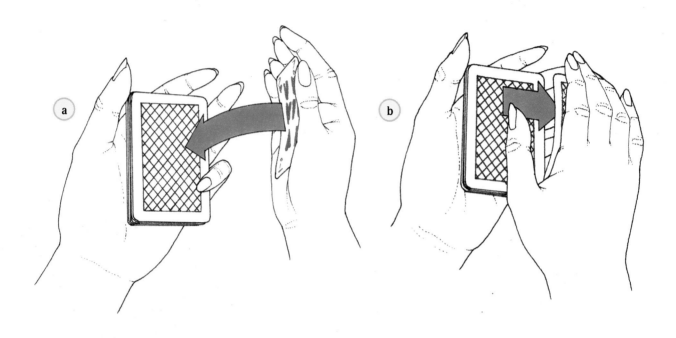

Effect: The magician calls for two volunteers and asks one to stand on each side of her. She turns to volunteer A, giving him the deck, and asks him to count out 10 cards onto her extended left hand. Once he has done this, she tucks the packet into his front pocket, and takes back the deck. Turning to volunteer B, she asks him to repeat the same process, and then has him tuck the packet into *his* front pocket. She asks both if they are sure they counted their cards right; then suggests that volunteer B is less certain of this than volunteer A, so that it might be a good idea if he checked. He finds that he has only nine cards. "I suppose you think I pinched it?" says the magician. To prove her innocence, she counts out the remaining cards in the deck – 32, just as it should be. She then turns an accusing finger towards volunteer A: "It was you, wasn't it?" Sure enough, it proves that volunteer A has 11 cards.

Method: The deception is simply palming (see page 17).

a) Before handing the deck to volunteer A, palm the top card into your right hand.

b) Transfer the counted cards from your left hand to your right, adding the extra one, as you put the packet in volunteer A's pocket. Later, once volunteer B has counted his cards, again transfer them from left hand to right before giving them back to him, and this time palm off one of the cards from his packet. Receive the deck from him with your left hand and immediately transfer it to your right.

TIP

The second act of palming is the one in which you are most likely to be caught. Use distraction. Start as if to tuck the packet into his pocket, as you did with volunteer A, then "change your mind", saying something like "Oh, you're a grown-up. You can do this yourself" as you transfer the packet back from right to left hand to give to him. In almost the same movement, *take the deck from his free hand* rather than wait to be offered it; this will startle him enough that he will not notice what else might be going on.

◆ Boxing Back

Effect: The magician pulls a deck from its box and offers the fanned cards to a volunteer, asking him to pick one. The card he chooses is returned to the deck, which is then thoroughly shuffled and returned to the box, which is placed under a handkerchief. The magician then pauses, saying, "I want you to be absolutely certain there's no trickery involved here – just magic." She retrieves the box from under the handkerchief, pulls out the face-down deck and asks the volunteer to count the cards to make sure they are all there. Once he has satisfied himself that there are indeed still 52 cards, she returns the deck to its box once more, puts the box under the handkerchief and guesses that his card was the Six of Diamonds. "No," he replies, "it was the . . ." But she stops him. "Let's try this again," she says, once more reaching for the box; but just before she removes the handkerchief she says, "Oh, silly me. What I meant to say was [e.g.,] the Seven of Hearts." She pulls the deck from the box and spreads out the cards face-down to show that the Seven of Hearts is the only card which is face-up among them.

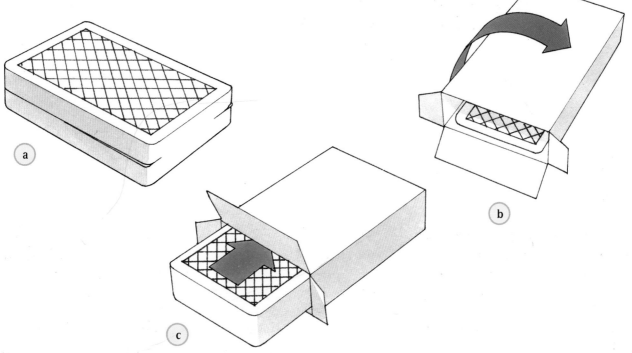

Method: This trick involves shaved cards. Using a vice or otherwise, you have beforehand prepared the deck by trimming off its long edges at a slight angle; once both edges have been trimmed (using a scalpel or sandpaper) the cards taper, being wider at one end than at the other.

a) Make sure that all the cards are initially the same way, but turn the deck as the volunteer replaces the chosen card, so that its corners protrude from those of the rest of the cards. Insert the deck into the box in this same direction. When you remove the deck the first time, grip the box between your thumb and first finger so that the chosen card is retained in place as the others are pulled out; if you have longish fingernails, you can wrap those of thumb and first finger over the edges of the opening to trap the chosen card in place.

b) Turn the "empty" box over as you put it down, so that the chosen card is now face-up.

c) When you next return the deck, face-down, you can catch a glimpse of this card, which you should make sure is pushed somewhere into the middle of the deck. The volunteer's count comes to 52 because (unknown to the volunteer) you started off with 53 cards, using an extra one drawn from an identical deck.

♣ SHORT SHRIFT

Effect: The magician asks a volunteer to select any card from the deck and to examine it. She tells him to put the card on top of the deck, which she immediately cuts, so that the chosen card is now somewhere in the middle. "You could do that as well as me," she says, inviting him to cut the deck himself a couple of times. She then requests that he blindfold her as securely as he is able. Blindfolded, she suggests he cuts the deck a couple more times – "You're getting good at this, aren't you?" – and then give it to her. Squaring it up on the table in front of her, she riffles its ends once or twice (see page 16) and then pulls from it the chosen card.

Method: For this trick you require a short card – i.e., a card faked by having had a tiny amount or so shaved off each end – or a thick card.

a) In normal use a short card will be indistinguishable from its fellows, but when it is in the squared-up deck the shortfall can be easily detected – if you are feeling for it. A thick card – most easily made by gluing an old card to the back of one of the cards in the deck you plan to use – does not have the advantage of being usable for other purposes. Either type of gimmicked card makes a distinct *click* when you riffle the deck.

♥ TWISTING CARD

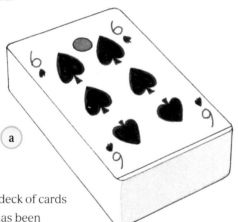

Effect: The magician produces a deck of cards through one end of which a hole has been punched. She asks a volunteer to choose a card and return it to the deck. Shuffling, she goes to her table and picks up a length of ribbon, which she passes to the volunteer for checking. She then threads the ribbon through the hole and asks him to tie the loose ends tightly. She fans out the cards for one last check, blindfolds him (or has a second volunteer do that for her), then puts the knot in his hand, letting the deck hang beneath. She says: "You know what your card is but can't see it; it's about time you let the rest of us see it, even though we don't know what it is." She asks him to give the ribbon a jerk, and one card is discovered to have reversed itself in the deck. On removal of his blindfold, the volunteer confirms that this is indeed his card.

Method: You can use any of the forcing techniques (pages 20–22) to make sure his selection is (say) the Six of Spades.

a) This particular Six of Spades has been drawn from an identical deck and has had its end (the opposite end from the hole) shaved off as described for the preceding trick.

b) While he is examining it, palm (see page 17) the top card of the deck and surreptitiously turn the deck over, returning the palmed card face-down to the top of the now face-up deck.

c) Splay the deck a little as you offer it to him for him to push his card back in. When you return to your table, again palm off the reversed top card and unobtrusively dump it or reverse it.

b) At the start of this trick, have the short or thick card at the bottom of the deck, and keep it there as you shuffle. The effect of the first cut is thus to put the faked card directly over the chosen one, and this relationship will remain no matter how often the deck is cut subsequently. Just before the denouement, make sure the deck is well squared – i.e., do this bit yourself – and then riffle the deck's ends with your thumbnail.

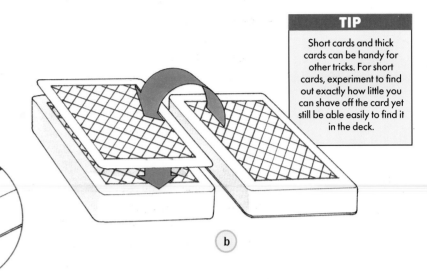

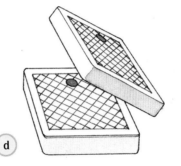

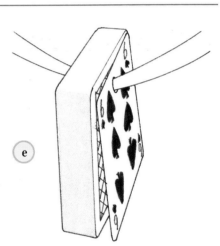

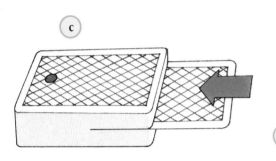

> **TIP**
>
> Short cards and thick cards can be handy for other tricks. For short cards, experiment to find out exactly how little you can shave off the card yet still be able easily to find it in the deck.

> **TIP**
>
> This trick operates much better with ribbon (as described) than with string. White ribbon makes the extra loop around the end of the Six much less noticeable than would any other color.

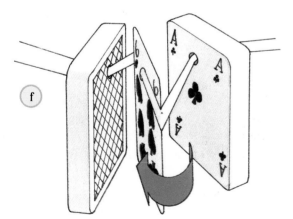

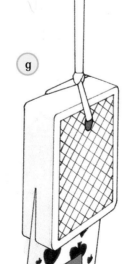

d) Cut the deck casually at the point indicated by the short card, as if it were easier to maneuver the ribbon through two halves rather than the whole deck at once.

e) Carefully thread the lower half, including the face-up Six.

f) Then thread the upper half, but have some slight difficulty just as you are finishing, so that

with your non-ribbon hand you can rotate the doctored Six, turning it face-down like all the others. Grip the deck tightly while the volunteer ties the knot, and tug against him to tighten the loop of ribbon around the turned card. Hereafter he is the only person who might notice the loop, which is why you have him blindfolded.

g) The rest of the trick works itself.

♠ TEARING A LADY IN HALF

Effect: The magician pulls the Queen of Spades from the deck, holds the card up and announces that she is about to perform a card variant of the classic trick, Sawing a Lady in Half. So saying, she slowly and deliberately tears the Queen in half. Then she says that she will go one better: quite openly, so that the audience can see exactly what she is doing, she puts the two halves one over the other and tears them again – she has Torn the Lady in Quarters. She holds up all four quarters in (say) her left hand for everyone to see. Pulling a folded handkerchief from her top pocket with her right hand, she drapes it over her left hand and reminds the audience that the difficult part of the original trick was not the actual

sawing of the lady in half – *anyone* can do that – but restoring her afterward. So saying, she whips the handkerchief away to reveal the restored Queen. Both card and handkerchief can then be examined.

Method: You use two Queens from identical decks. The second Queen is inside the folded handkerchief, which you grip between finger and thumb (holding the card through the cloth) as you shake it out. As a continuation of the movement of shaking, drape the handkerchief over the outstretched hand, depositing the whole card on top of the torn pieces. Your continued patter allows you to use the thumb and fingers of

♦ CONFORMIST JACK

Effect: The magician picks the Jack of Spades from the deck and tells the audience that this is well known by all students of cards to be the most conformist of any of the 52. "You wouldn't think so just to look at it," she remarks, passing it to the front row so that they can indeed look at it. Taking the card back, and with the deck held back-out toward the audience, its long edges upward, she pushes the Jack, face-out, down through the deck until its bottom part protrudes below. Turning the deck over, though still keeping it back-out to the audience, she pushes the Jack back through it, but this time it emerges back-out like the other cards, having "conformed". Again the Jack can be inspected by the audience.

Method: Cut the Jack of Spades from another deck in half horizontally, and have one of the halves palmed (see page 17) face-down in (say) your left hand.

a) While the whole Jack is being inspected, palm the face-down top card of the deck in your right hand, turn the deck over and place the palmed card face-down on the deck, which is otherwise face-up in your left hand with the half-

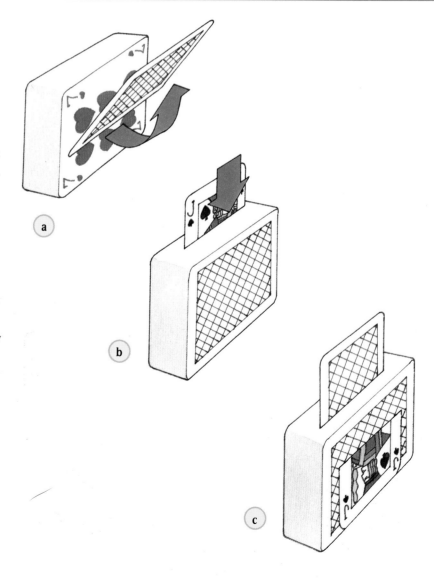

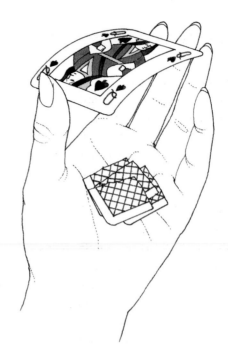

the left hand, hidden by the handkerchief, to edge the whole card toward the thumb side of that hand and the torn pieces towards the facing side; the whole card should end up lying like a bridge across the gap between thumb and first two fingers. When you whip the handkerchief away, do it quickly, and take with it the four fragments. Tuck the handkerchief loosely into a side pocket, out of the way (dropping the fragments into that pocket as you do so), ostensibly so that you can use both hands to hold up the "restored" card. Pass the card around the audience for inspection and, as if by afterthought, pull out the handkerchief so that it can be thoroughly examined as well.

> **TIP**
>
> If you are concerned that tucking the handkerchief into a pocket might seem too obvious, or that the audience might demand to examine the pocket as well, when picking up the fragments make sure to hold them between thumb and fingers near the handkerchief's hem. Retain both handkerchief and fragments in your right hand. Give out the card for examination: then, to give out the handkerchief, pull it naturally from the right hand with the left. You can then ditch the fragments.

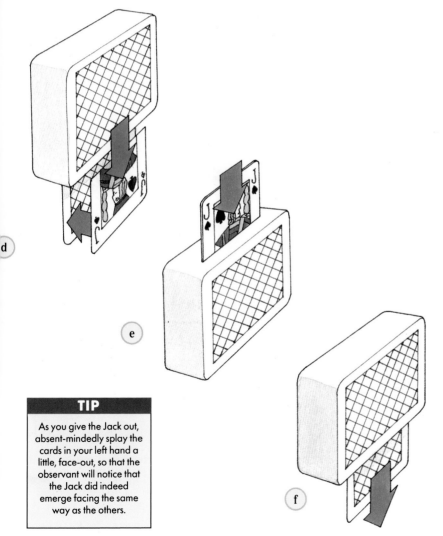

d)

e)

f)

> **TIP**
>
> As you give the Jack out, absent-mindedly splay the cards in your left hand a little, face-out, so that the observant will notice that the Jack did indeed emerge facing the same way as the others.

card at its rear. Holding the deck face-out in your left hand, you can keep the half-card at the rear of the deck with the left hand's first finger.

b & c) Push the Jack downward through the deck; it will look as if it is the only face-out card in the back-out deck. Push the Jack well through, and tug it an extra little bit with the right hand.

d) While giving the extra tug, use the right thumb to transfer the half-card to the rear of the protruding Jack, then start pushing the Jack upward, simultaneously pushing the half-card a little into the deck. When turning the deck over, it is easy enough to turn it around at the same time – just perform the action flamboyantly, and the extra move will go unnoticed.

e) The audience will think they are still seeing the face of the Jack, but in fact it is that of the half-card, with part of the Jack behind it.

f) Start pushing downward again, and the real Jack will emerge, having apparently reversed itself while going through the deck. Give the Jack out for examination and put the deck "carelessly" on your table, spilling it a little. If anyone calls to inspect the deck, pick it up equally "carelessly", losing the half-card and "fumblingly" turning over the reversed card.

♣ FILL THE GAP

Effect: The magician puts a deck on her table and turns her back. She asks a volunteer to draw four cards from the deck and lay them out left to right in a row, face-down. Still with her back turned, she asks him to go back to his place and that another volunteer should come forward and select one card from the face-down row; this card (e.g., the Five of Hearts) he should display to the audience as a whole and then put back in its place. The magician then calls for a third volunteer to gather up the four cards in order and bring them to her; she sends him away, studies the cards, puts one of them in her breast pocket, and calls for a fourth volunteer to come and collect the remaining three cards from her and to lay them out in a row, as before, but with a gap in place of the missing card. For the first time she turns around to face the audience. Glancing at the depleted row of cards on the table, she pulls the fourth card from her pocket and places it face-up in the gap that was left. Sure enough, it is the Five of Hearts.

♥ UNRELIABLE JUMBO

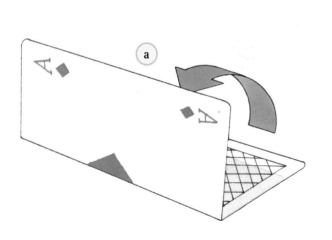

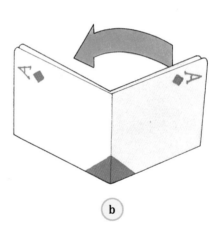

Effect: The magician explains that – because they think it improves their showmanship – a lot of other magicians have taken to using Jumbo Cards, which are just like ordinary playing cards but very much bigger. She herself chooses not to, not just because she is a traditionalist, not just because Jumbo Cards are incredibly expensive, not just because she keeps dropping them every time she tries to use them, but because . . . well, Jumbo Cards are *unreliable*: they do things you are not expecting them to do. She produces one to demonstrate, showing it front and back. She holds it up face-out to the audience, slowly folds it in half, folds it in half again, then again; then she unfolds it equally slowly to show that the Jumbo Card has turned around, so that it is now back-out to the audience. "I rest my case," she says, tossing it to the audience for inspection while she turns to start the next trick.

Method: At the outset, you already have three random cards from the deck in your breast pocket. Any time after you have turned your back, you can use the distraction of volunteers being called and dismissed to bring these three cards out. While you are telling the audience that you are putting a single card into the pocket, in fact you put there all four of the cards that were brought from the table. When you turn, the position of the gap immediately tells you the position of the selected card. You reach into your pocket, find the right card with your thumbnail, and draw it forth as if it were the sole card there.

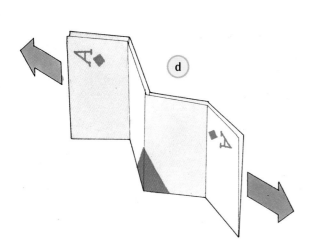

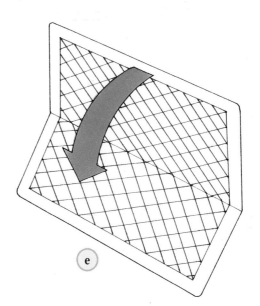

Method: There is no real deception involved, and the Jumbo Card is not faked in any way. The folding and unfolding run as follows (with right–left directions reversed if you are left-handed):

a) First fold the Jumbo Card lengthways, turning the bottom half up toward you.

b) Now fold it vertically in half from left to right, folding toward you.

c) Now fold it vertically in half from left to right again, but this time folding toward the audience.

d) Taking the pair of cut ends closest to you, straighten out the folded card in one movement, so that the only fold remaining is the longitudinal one.

e) Straighten it out as well, and the back of the Jumbo Card is now seen to be facing the audience. The effect is quite startling, because it is only with this final unfolding that they see the back of the card for the first time.

♠ THE SHEEP FROM THE GOATS

Effect: The magician shuffles the deck and then asks a volunteer to do likewise – and, for good measure, to have the deck shuffled by a couple of other people from the audience as well. While this shuffling is in progress, the magician writes a prediction on a sheet of paper and passes it, folded a couple of times, to someone in the front row, with instructions that he is on no account to look at it. She then asks the volunteer to deal out the shuffled deck in pairs: if he turns up two red cards they should go on one heap, if two black cards they should go on another, while mismatched pairs should be discarded. Once he has done this, she asks him to total up the number of cards in the red heap and the number in the black heap. Finally she calls on the person with the piece of paper to stand up and read her prediction out loud: "You will have two more red cards than you have black." The volunteer confirms that this is indeed the case.

♦ KINGS ON TOP

Effect: The magician tells the audience how she is a monarchist at heart, because it's a sad but true fact of life that royal breeding does tell: a prince may change places with a pauper but, whatever Mark Twain said, it will always be easy to distinguish the one from the other. By way of demonstration she shuffles the deck and then passes it to a volunteer, asking him to cut it into four approximately equal heaps. She then asks him to move cards about seemingly at random from one heap to another – "Take three cards from that heap and put it on that one. Now, take two cards from this heap and put one of them on that heap and the other over here" – until everyone has lost track of everything. She then suddenly claps her hands, says that's plenty, and asks him to turn over the top card of each heap: sure enough, they prove to be the four Kings, "who will always end up at the top of the heap, no matter what happens".

Method: Earlier, you arranged for all four Kings to be at the top of the deck, and during your shuffling you simply keep them there. When the volunteer cuts the deck into four heaps, make sure you know which heap has the four Kings at its top. The various transpositions you then instruct the volunteer to perform have the object of moving the Kings to the places you desire. Precisely what those transpositions are is up to you: you can vary them each time you perform the trick. All that you have to do is keep track of the Kings, which is a lot simpler than it seems – try it with a friend a few times beforehand.

TIP

You can adapt this trick, using Jacks instead of Kings, to form the denouement of The Scurvy Knaves (1) — see page 48.

Method: This is laughably easy: all you need to do is remove any two of the black cards from the deck before starting. If the audience paused to think about it, they would realize that you must have done this, as otherwise there would have to be equal numbers of cards in the red and black heaps. However, the complication of the pairing for the discard heap, plus your flow of patter, will be enough to ensure that the audience *don't* think about this!

TIP

You can of course set things up so that instead there are two more black cards than red, or four or six more of one color than of the other. It is wise, however, not to go for numbers higher than this (even six is a bit risky) and certainly not to opt for an odd number as the difference — that would seem so unnatural that the audience would immediately realize the deception.

♣ KINGS ON QUEENS ON TOP

Effect: Using roughly the same patter as for the preceding trick, the magician shuffles the cards and passes the deck to a volunteer, asking him to cut it into four roughly equal heaps. She issues him a complex set of instructions to move cards around between the four heaps, then finally claps her hands, says that's plenty, and asks him to turn up the top card of each heap. These four cards prove to be the four Kings. However, before the applause starts, she sets the Kings to one side, quietens the audience, and issues the volunteer another set of instructions. At the end of these she again claps her hands and asks him to turn over the next card on each heap. These prove to be the four Queens.

Method: At the outset you have arranged that the four Kings and four Queens are at the top of the deck, and you retain them there as you shuffle. Thereafter, all you are really doing is performing the preceding trick twice in a row. Keep things reasonably simple for the first part of this trick – you do not want to disturb the little "nest" of Queens at the top of one heap. During the second part of the trick, that heap may start to look a little too obviously smaller than the rest; your first instruction of the second set might therefore be to move four cards (i.e., the four Queens) from that heap to another.

TIP

It is nice to be able to use this trick as a follow-up to the preceding one – but the difficulty is that you require a fresh stacked deck. One way round this – assuming money is no object – is, at the end of the preceding trick, to give the deck you have used to the volunteer as a souvenir. It seems natural, as you draw a fresh deck for the new trick, to call also for a fresh volunteer – who, of course, must at the end of the trick likewise be given the deck as a keepsake.

♥ ACES

Effect: The magician holds up the deck face-out to the audience, and then deals out two heaps of cards face-down, one heap for herself and the other for a volunteer. Both face the audience. Putting the rest of the deck to one side, she takes her own packet and puts it behind her back, asking the volunteer to do the same. She says that both will jumble the cards behind their backs as much as they want, although keeping the cards face-down; then, when the volunteer is satisfied, still keeping the rest of her packet behind her back she brings forward a card (face-down) from it, which she offers in exchange for one he draws from the packet behind his own back. She asks the volunteer to insert the card she has given him into his own packet *face-up*, still behind his back, while she does likewise with the card she has taken from him. Now they produce the two packets and fan them out face-down with (obviously) the two exchanged cards showing face-up. These prove both to be Aces, the one in the volunteer's hand being black and the other one red. This seems a great coincidence, but then the magician turns her fan around to show that all her other cards are black, while all the other cards in the volunteer's hand prove to be red.

♠ FLEEING RED

Effect: The magician deals out a number of black cards – all the black cards in the deck, if she likes. Lastly, she deals out any red card at random. Gathering up the cards, she shuffles them a few times to show that there is still only one poor, sad, lonely red card (e.g., the Ten of Diamonds) in their midst. She squares up the packet, pulls out a handkerchief and calls for a volunteer. The one she chooses is near the back, and as he is making his way forward she reassures him: "There's no need to be frightened – all I'm going to do is this." Then she gives a demonstration. She takes the packet in one hand, drapes the handkerchief over it with the other, holds the packet loosely through the cloth, and then swiftly pulls the handkerchief away. When he arrives she gives him the packet and tells him to hold it really tightly. She then shakes out the handkerchief, drapes it over the deck, and swiftly pulls the handkerchief away. Giving the handkerchief to him, she asks him to look at the cards, and, yes, the Ten has vanished. "The Ten," she announces, "has now fled to my jacket pocket . . . oh, dear, this wasn't supposed to happen . . ." She only now realizes that she took

off her jacket earlier in the routine and draped it over a chair. Telling the volunteer to put the cards and handkerchief down, she asks him to go and have a look in her jacket top pocket, meanwhile worrying aloud that she doesn't think the Ten could possibly have fled such a distance: "Cards have *very* short legs, you know." However, the volunteer finds the Ten there, sure enough.

Method: This trick requires a stacked deck. Decide how many cards you want in each packet – e.g., 12 – and arrange the top 21 cards (i.e., twice 12 = 24, minus 3 = 21) alternately red and black: the values of the cards do not matter, but should be as haphazard as possible. The 22nd card should be a black Ace and the 24th a red Ace, with the 23rd being any other red card. Put the packet of 24 cards on top of the rest of the deck: the ordering will not be apparent when you fan the whole deck out briefly in front of the audience. Dealing out the cards will ensure that the volunteer has all red cards and that you have 10 black cards plus a black Ace and a red Ace, in that order. While the volunteer is jumbling his cards, you look as if you are doing likewise; in fact you are taking the red Ace from the top of your packet, turning it around, and slipping it face-up into the middle of your packet. The card you offer the volunteer is of course the black Ace. When you take his card behind your back, ostensibly to turn it face-up and push it into your packet, you in fact shove it into a convenient pocket or waistband.

TIP

It is a good idea to have plenty of royal cards – not too many! – in the stacked section: their colors will further distract the audience's eyes from the red–black alternation. If you are worried that someone might notice that, at the end, there is one fewer card in your fan than in the volunteer's, slightly alter your original stacking and give yourself two cards in the guise of one at the end of the deal.

(b)

(c)

Method: For this trick you need a deck of tapering shaved cards – as described for Boxing Back (see page 67) – plus an extra Ten of Diamonds from an unshaved deck. Plant the shaved Ten in your jacket top pocket beforehand; the unshaved one you put into the deck, and obviously this is the red card you select "at random". The deception occurs when you are demonstrating to the volunteer what you want him to do.

a) Holding the deck fairly loosely, grip the edges of the Ten through the handkerchief.

b) Then you can take it away as you whip the handkerchief away.

c) Holding the handkerchief casually with one hand at your stomach, gesticulate with the deck in the other hand toward the advancing volunteer; this will misdirect attention enough for you to slip the Ten inside your shirt. Thereafter the trick works itself, but do bully the volunteer into holding the deck very tightly, so that he knows you cannot have taken the Ten from it!

TIP

Experiment, and if you find the edges of the undoctored Ten are insufficiently raised from those of the shaved packet for you to get a confident grip, instead put the plain Ten in your jacket and have the shaved one in the deck. While dealing, make sure you keep all the black cards with the taper in the same direction; the red card, being separately selected, can be tossed "casually" on top of them, giving it a slight spin as you toss it, so that it lies with its taper in the opposite direction from the others.

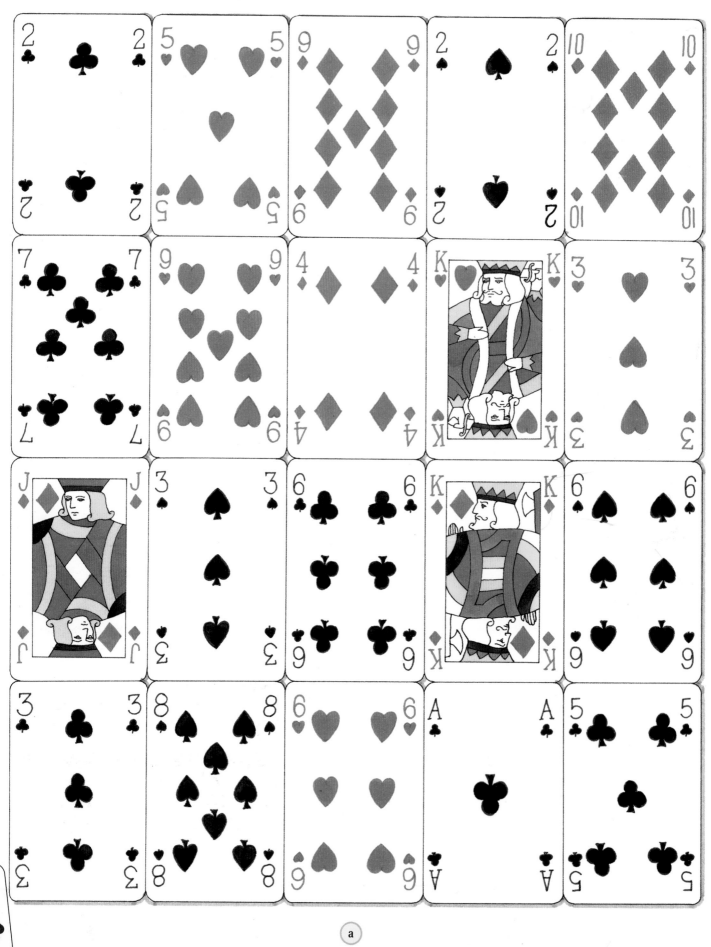

◆ Mutus Nomen Cocis Dedit

Effect: The magician asks a volunteer to shuffle the deck and then to deal from it the top 20 cards in the form of 10 pairs; the remainder of the deck is put to one side. He must then decide on one of the pairs, but not tell the magician which that is. She then gathers together the 20 cards and sets them out on the table in random order in four rows of five, and asks the volunteer to locate the now separated cards of his pair, but again not to tell her which they are; instead, all she asks is that he divulge the row or rows in which the two cards appear. As soon as he does so, she is able to identify the cards.

Method: This trick depends on your remembering a piece of dog Latin: *Mutus Nomen Cocis Dedit.*

a) When you are laying out the 20 cards, the order in which you do so is not random at all. Instead you imagine that the letters of the Latin words are laid out in front of you:

```
M  U  T  U  S
N  O  M  E  N
C  O  C  I  S
D  E  D  I  T
```

Place the first card at the top left corner of this imaginary grid, in the position denoted "M"; the second card goes at the center of the second row, in the other position denoted "M". The next two cards go in the two positions denoted "U", and so on until the grid is complete.

b) The information as to the row or rows in which the two cards appear is, as you can see, sufficient for you to identify the volunteer's pair.

TIP

For the best effect, ask several volunteers mentally to select pairs of cards – as many volunteers as you wish. The fact that you can determine a single pair of cards from the given information is only moderately impressive; that you can do it several times, at speed, is what really gives the impression of magic.

♣ CHEATING

Effect: The magician offers out a deck to the audience and tells them to pass it around among themselves, with three (or four, or five) people each taking a single card from it; those volunteers, once they have selected both themselves and their cards, must stand up, each holding his card so that the magician cannot see it. She accepts back the residue of the deck and returns to her table, where she puts on a blindfold.

a) Picking up the deck and moving warily to the front of the stage, she asks the volunteers to come to her. Once they are beside her, she riffles the deck (see page 16), asking the first volunteer to call out where she should stop riffling so that he may insert his card. She repeats the process with the other volunteers, then gives the deck a thorough shuffle. She begins dealing out the cards face-down, but suddenly stops and announces that the next card is one of the chosen ones. She gives it to the volunteer whose card it was, then continues until she finds another of the chosen cards, and another, and . . .

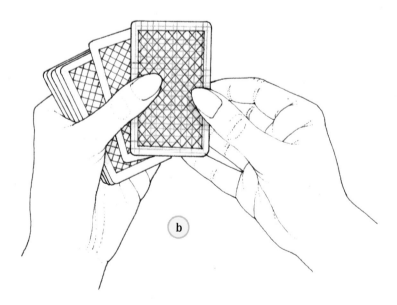

Method: This trick is really a cheat. It is possible to buy good-quality cards in two finishes: one plain, the other "linen".

b) The difference is not very obvious to the eye but is clearly detectable by the fingertips. The deck you pass around the audience should have the "linen" finish. When you return to your table to put on the blindfold, you quite naturally have to put the deck down to leave yourself both hands free. The deck you pick up is identical in every respect with the original except that the cards have the plain style of finish. The volunteers might spot the difference if they were able to see the faces of the cards, which is why you keep hold of the deck while they insert their cards.